CW01647511

MÖTLEY CRÜE
RED, WHITE AND CRUE TOUR 2005
with very
SPECIAL GUESTS
motörhead
& THE CASANOVAS
Sat 3 Dec - SYDNEY Superdome
Sun 4 Dec - BRISBANE Entertainment Centre
Tues 6 Dec - MELBOURNE Vodafone Arena

Collect these other Mötley Crüe books by Paul Miles:

Chronological Crue Vol. 1 - The Eighties
The complete history of Mötley Crüe in the 1980s

Chronological Crue Vol. 2 - The Nineties
The complete history of Mötley Crüe in the 1990s

Chronological Crue Vol. 3 - The Naughties
The complete history of Mötley Crüe in the 2000s

Chronological Crue Vol. 4 - The Onesies
The ongoing history of Mötley Crüe in the 2010s

What Mötley Crüe Means to Me
Crüeheads Share Their Stories

Lots more in the world of Mötley Crüe at the Chronological Crue website:

www.CrueTime.com

MÖTLEY CRÜE DOWN UNDER

On Tour with The Carnival of Sins

PAUL MILES

First edition published 2006.
This second edition, published by:

Chronological Crue
GPO Box 2220
Melbourne Victoria 3001
Australia

Email: milestone1183@yahoo.com
Web: www.CrueTime.com

Chronological Crue is a publishing entity of Paul Miles,
ABN 21 790 841 870

Printed with chlorine-free ink on acid-free interior paper stock, made from 30% post-consumer waste recycled material. Manufactured on-demand to reduce any excess production.

ISBN 978-1-7955-3961-6

"When your trash becomes your treasure, your immorals are my pleasure. Lose your mind at your leisure."

Sick Love Song, Mötley Crüe, 2005.

Contents

Introduction

A big job, but someone had to do it: It was my duty and absolute pleasure to don my clown suit and open each and every one of the 140-odd Mötley Crüe performances during 2005.

Therefore it seems only natural that after hanging-out down under in Australia with Paul Miles for the six Crüe concerts in eight days that I also begin this entertaining book of his tour adventures for you.

So Crüeheads, what's it like to tour with those crazy Mötley guys? Read on for a unique insight into life on the road with The Carnival of Sins. I just hope Paul doesn't tell you any tall stories about me falling asleep at that strip club…

'Mighty Mike' Murga
www.mightymike.tv

Foreplay

It all began in December 2004 when the original members of Mötley Crüe reunited for a press conference, announcing a string of new tour dates for their 'Red, White & Crüe 2005...Better Live Than Dead' tour. They promised Australia was on the list of places they were to play but the fans down under had heard that before in years gone by.

However, this time it felt different to me. Just four months earlier I had met Nikki Sixx for the first time, and as I drove him through Melbourne city, he told me that he wanted to bring the Crüe here next year. His best intentions aside, I had been let down before and have hoped for Mötley to tour Australia for too many years to let his seemingly off-the-cuff comment get me excited. But as the new year of 2005 kicked off, his words began to turn into reality.

As January began, I was contacted by Petrina Convey, the Product Manager at Universal Music Australia assigned to marketing the band's Red, White & Crüe release in Australia. She told me, "I've been having a bit of a search online for Australian Mötley websites and yours is by far the best so I thought I should send an email and touch base with you." Gee I love the Internet, I thought. "We're currently putting a plan together and we'd obviously like to get the Australian fans involved in any way we can. We'd love to have you involved with this project so I look forward to speaking with you soon!" A great relationship developed from there as we worked together on various projects, as she executed her plan.

Just a few weeks later, Petrina said, "At this stage we have no guarantee that the band will be coming out here so we really need to get a petition happening to highlight to the band and local promoters that there is still a large fan-base out here." I got on board and offered to kickstart the petition to Bring the Crüe to Australia. We needed to move fast.

Petrina organised for Tommy Lee to be interviewed via satellite by Rove McManus on his high-profile Australian entertainment show Rove Live on Tuesday, February 8. She instructed Rove's production staff to ensure that Rove said the following to end the interview segment: "Paul Miles from the Australian Mötley Crüe website Chronological Crue has organised a petition to bring the Crüe out to Australia. Fans need to log onto www.fasterlouder.com.au and sign the petition to get the band out here."

As we watched the television interview draw to a close that night, there was unfortunately no such plug from Rove. Petrina was not a happy camper! They didn't even mention the fact that the petition was online. She specifically asked them to announce it and they just didn't do it. What the?

The video clip for If I Die Tomorrow then started to get a small amount of airplay on Australian television, as thousands of petition signatures rolled in. The band was now kicking ass on the road in North America and on the last day of February, Petrina told me the great news that Tommy Lee was possibly coming out to Australia for the Jack Awards in May and that he would most likely be announcing a Mötley Crüe tour of Australia at that time.

The Melbourne nightclub that I was regularly DJing at, Back in the Day, held an official Red, White & Crüe album launch. The record company provided copies of the double-disc to give away, along with other Mötley promotional items. I got a little taste of what it's like to be a member of Mötley Crüe when I told the 300-plus crowd that it seemed the Crüe were coming and they needed to practice for Tommy's tittie cam. Many ladies exposed their tits in the direction of my DJ booth and got very excited when I passed down CD prizes to them on the dance floor. I then cranked the revving motorbike intro of Girls, Girls, Girls as the song got them grooving again.

March soon ticked away and the Jack Awards in Sydney drew closer, with the guest appearance by Tommy firmed up in April. I emailed Tommy, saying, "I live in Melbourne but could fly up to Sydney if you're not coming down here… if you wanna hang for a bit?" He replied, "Yup, I'll be there from the 7th-17th."

As May arrived, I was soon proofing A2 poster and DL card artwork for the promoter and their marketing agents, pointing out errors including the incorrect spelling of a band member's name. I spoke with the tour publicist Chrissie Camp on the phone who asked that I email her some thoughts for the press release announcing the tour. I offered that I would be pleased to cast an eye over anything else for verification; I know that fans hate errors of course.

Chrissie did a great job with the press release and I soon had a copy ready to forward to the fans. The release was to be sent to media on Sunday, May 8, but I was able to break the news to my subscribers the night before, commencing my email with, "Ooh! Are you ready boys? Are you ready girls? We did it! Our 'Bring the Crüe to Australia' petition was successful – Mötley is coming down under in December. Here's the official word for you – fuck yeah."

> **Media Release, Sunday May 8**
> **MOTLEY CRUE ON THEIR WAY!**
> **'RED, WHITE AND CRUE' AUSTRALIAN TOUR ANNOUNCED**
>
> UK'S MOTORHEAD NAMED AS SPECIAL GUESTS
>
> It's now official! The original members of Motley Crue, the raucous rulers of the sex-and-drugs-fueled nightlife on LA's Sunset Strip and one of the world's most infamous rock bands, will bring their "Red, White & Crue Tour 2005" to Australian shores in December.
>
> The tour is announced to coincide with the promo visit by drummer Tommy Lee, the VIP guest at the May 10 Jack Awards in Sydney.

Re-uniting the band's classic original lineup - Nikki Sixx, Vince Neil, Mick Mars and Tommy Lee – the reunion tour has been outrageously successful and this is the news Australian fans have been waiting for!

Featuring a three-ring circus of freaks under a huge big top set, complete with a fire-breathing midget as the MC, sexy acrobats, flying drum kits and enough pyro to light up a small city, we're talking good old-fashioned low morals, glam metal rock'n'roll!!

"The entire event was a chance to let loose one's inner evil clown. There's little else that dares to be so brazen, so obvious, so obsessed with the pleasures of the moment" (Edmonton Sun)
"Big, loud and dirty!" (Mtv.com)
"The feel-good reunion of the year" (Entertainment Weekly)
"Evidently there is life after death. And it's a hell of a (freak) show" (NME)
"Pop and hair metal glory" (Beacon Journal)
"Wonderfully entertaining" (Ottawa Sun)
"One of the best heavy metal arena shows you'll likely see in this day and age" (Calgary Sun)
"An unqualified success" (Boston Herald)
"My rating - four devil horns" (Philadelphia Inquirer)
Get the picture? This tour is HOT!

We all know the Motley Crue story. They built a rabid glam-metal following in their '80s LA heyday with a string of hit albums "Too Fast For Love", "Shout At The Devil", "Theatre Of Pain", "Girls Girls Girls" and "Dr Feelgood", and sold out stadiums to the tune of 10 million concert tickets.

Yet all the forces that made Motley Crue's kick-ass music so authentic, namely their own reckless lifestyle of excess, gradually took its toll. In 1987 Nikki Sixx was revived after flatlining from a heroin overdose.

Add to that brawls, lawsuits and just about every other shenanigan you can think of, and no wonder their official biography "The Dirt" is recognised by many as one of the best rock books ever written.

Fast-forward six years and under the relentless persistence of a UK promoter, the band is back in the saddle. And, as one journalist noted, with the world gone crazy, what better time for a good-time shot in the arm of anthemic glam metal.

Joining the Crue to make this a hellishly hard rockin' night will be evergreen UK band Motorhead. Celebrating 25 years since the release of their debut "Ace Of Spades", Lemmy and the boys got the best reviews of their career for last year's fantastic "Inferno" album. This year they were awarded a Grammy for Best Metal Performance and are in rip-snorting form.

Winning the eagerly-sort after Aussie opening spot are The Casanovas, well on their way to being one of the best live acts in the country. With a great new single "Heartbeat", and a lengthy o/s tour upcoming, by December they will be red hot.

So there you have it, the Crue, Motorhead and The Casanovas. If you can't rock to this, you're dead.

Saturday December 3, Sydney Superdome, Ticketek 132 849
Sunday December 4, Brisbane Entertainment Centre, Ticketek 132 849
Tuesday December 6, Melbourne Vodafone Arena, Ticketek 132 849
Thursday December 8, Adelaide Entertainment Centre, BASS 131 246

TICKETS ON SALE FOR ALL SHOWS MONDAY MAY 23

With the press release now out, I packed a bag and caught a plane to Sydney. Upon arrival, I headed to the Universal Music offices and met Petrina in person for the first time. She gave me a little kit-box for the invitation-only 2005 Jack Awards event, consisting of a wristband, access pass and rock kaleidoscope. I was keen to hook up with Tommy during the day but his hectic schedule in Sydney was chock-full of promotional media obligations, making it extremely difficult for me to spend any time with him.

I eventually caught up with him at the InterContinental hotel, where he was staying. He had just completed some interviews and was waiting for his vehicle to take him to a radio station for his next commitment in a moment. As he sat on the porter's luggage trolley and sipped a glass of white wine, I chatted with him for five minutes or so until he had to leave. The moment was gone in an instant and I wished it was longer, but I was pleased I had met Tommy in the flesh for the first time this Tuesday, May 10.

I headed back to my hotel and got ready for the awards night. My taxi dropped me across the road from the Seymour Centre in Chippendale and I saw searchlights panning the dark skies. The traditional red carpet was replaced with 'black carpet' and after showing my access pass to security I joined the other music industry people set to enjoy the celebration of Australian live rock music. It was exciting to be a part of it.

Ordering a Jack & Dry at the bar with a $20 note held out in my hand, I smiled when the barman told me that drinks were actually free all night. I saw some guys from the Hell City Glamours, having met them backstage the year before when they supported Brides of Destruction in Sydney, and we chatted as we headed downstairs and back out to the black carpet. Watching more musicians get interviewed by Channel V, I was eagerly awaiting the arrival of the night's special guest.

With a sudden flurry of media activity at the start of the black carpet, I knew the time had come. Looking like a pimp in his pinstriped suit, tie and hat, Tommy was flashed, snapped, and interviewed as he began his entry, while sipping on the Jack & Coke in his hand.

As the media frenzy died down further along the barricaded entry, I walked out on the black carpet and greeted Tommy, who seemed pleased that I was at the event, saying, "Hey bro, right on!" I took a photo of us with my camera before more television personalities confiscated him for a short interview.

As the commotion died down, everyone headed inside for the 9pm start of the awards ceremony, while sculling the Jacks that was not allowed in the auditorium. I saw my friend Bill Walsh (drummer of the Cosmic Psychos and owner of Melbourne's famous Cherry bar where I DJ), and his lady Jane Rocca (music journalist and author), so we watched the awards unfold together from the stalls.

Tommy was cool on stage as he presented a couple of awards and squirted Jack Daniels at the audience from two large super-soaker water pistols. The drinking soon began in the foyer again as the official proceedings came to a close. After a couple of hours worth of more free drinks, I asked Petrina if she knew what Tommy was up to since he hadn't joined the party; she didn't know.

They closed the bar on us at 1am, so I headed with Silverchair's Ben Gillies, Spiderbait's Kram and The Living End's Chris Cheney to another drinking establishment a few streets away. Using their beer stubbies as microphones, Ben and Kram sang a raucous version of Kickstart My Heart to me, as the frivolities continued on and on.

That pub closed too, forcing us to taxi it to another with Patch and Sarah McLeod from The Superjesus, and two barely-eighteen girls who had won a magazine competition to be flown to the event and were having the best time of their sweet young lives.

As 6am came around, I reluctantly thought I'd better leave the pub and my drinking mates. The birds were chirping as I greeted the sunny morning sky, stumbling along the Sydney streets back to my hotel in The Rocks. I'd no sooner closed my eyes when my alarm went off, forcing me to get up and check out of the place. With a couple of hours to kill before my early-afternoon flight home, I parked myself on the steps of the Sydney Opera House, unable to really move due to a shocking hangover kicking in. The drinks may have been free, but I was certainly paying for them now!

Once back in Melbourne, I emailed Tommy, saying, "It was great to finally meet up so we could say Gday. Spewing that we only got a few minutes Tues arvo before you had to bail for another interview. Here's a pic attached that I grabbed with you on arrival at the Jack Awards. Anyway, trust you enjoyed Hayman Island. I'll be traveling to all the Aussie shows in Dec, so hopefully we can have a chance to hang a bit more then." Tommy replied, "Likewise mate!!! Be well and I'll see ya in Dec!!!"

Tickets for the Crüe's Australian concerts went on sale and everyone seemed pleased with the initial figures, although the Adelaide and Brisbane markets were of course slower. I talked with band management in Los Angeles about the tour, giving some views on tactics to improve sales in those two markets. The announcement of a Perth show was not included with the initial dates, as venue issues required more work to be done to lock the only outdoor event in.

As June arrived, the record company asked me to let the Crüeheads heads know that the VH1 special Resurrecting: Mötley Crüe was to be shown on Friday, June 10 and Monday, June 13. The video clip for Sick Love Song was then aired on Rage and I was told that I could tell fans that there's a rumor that there may be a second Melbourne show announced. But in the first week of July, the publicist told me that it was now doubtful that there would be a second Melbourne concert.

As the month progressed, the second Melbourne show was then on again and it would be announced with the Perth show early in August. Street posters then erroneously went up in Melbourne four days or so before the announcement was made, causing a flurry of emails to my inbox. To make matters worse, the street posters had Sep 7 instead of Dec 7 as the concert date, so people thought the whole tour was now being moved forward and were in panic-mode. The street posters were corrected and I sent out the announcement of two more Australian concerts for the fans. Here are the releases for you:

Media Release, Wednesday August 10
MOTLEY CRUE TO ROCK THE PALAIS!

After selling out Vodafone Arena, Motley Crüe is giving Melbourne the chance to get real up close and personal with a one-off show at the Palais Theatre!

Andrew McManus Presents today announced the Crüe would be rockin' the Palais Theatre on Wednesday December 7, the night after their sold out Vodafone Arena show on Tuesday December 6.

The Palais show will feature a slightly scaled down version of their rip-snorting circus-themed arena spectacular, but hell, here's the chance to get real intimate with Tommy, Nikki, Vince and Mick in an encore performance that promises to be one of THE shows of the year!

Since announcing their Australian tour in May, the Crüe's outrageously successful reformation tour continues to go gang-busters. The band's "Red, White & Crüe" album is now certified US platinum having sold more than a million copies, the band are soon to be presented with their own Hollywood Hall Of Fame Star, a sensational double-live concert DVD is about to hit the stores with massive anticipation and everything is going so well the band are committed to recording a brand new studio album early next year!

The Crüe are giving young up and comers AIRBOURNE the chance to strut their stuff as the support act. With a healthy respect for the fine art of foot-to-the-floor rock'n'roll, AIRBOURNE are looking like part of the next wave of great Aussie rock.

Nothing further needs to be said. This is destined to be one of those shows we're all talking about down the track. Miss it at your peril.

Tickets prices are: A Reserve $149 inclusive and B Reserve $129 inclusive.

On sale from the Palais 03 9537 2444 and Ticketmaster7.com 136 100

TICKETS ON SALE MONDAY AUGUST 22.

Make a note of that date 'cos on Tuesday 23rd, you'll be tooooo late!

www.ampresents.com www.motleycrue.com

Media Release, Wednesday August 10
MOTLEY CRUE ON THEIR WAY TO PERTH! BLACKJACK EVENT SET TO ROCK CLAREMONT SHOWGROUNDS.

It's been buzzing for months, but it's now official. The original members of Motley Crüe, the raucous rulers of the sex-and-drugs-fueled nightlife on LA's Sunset Strip and one of the world's most infamous rock bands, are on their way to WA.

The Crüe are set to rock Perth in a huge outdoor concert at Claremont Showgrounds on Saturday December 10 to be called BLACKJACK. Far more than just a Motley Crüe concert, BLACKJACK is set to be the ultimate cocktail of glamour, sleaze, mind-blowing production & scorching guitars.

BLACKJACK will happen on two concert stages from 5pm – 10pm featuring six bands, all invited because they adhere to the true spirit of rock'n'roll. This hellishly hard rockin' night will feature the legendary

Motorhead, The Living End, Fireballs, The Casanovas and Day of the Dead.

But it's the re-united classic original Mötley Crüe lineup - Nikki Sixx, Vince Neil, Mick Mars and Tommy Lee – WA fans have been waiting for!

Featuring a three-ring circus of freaks under a huge big top set, complete with a fire-breathing midget as the MC, sexy acrobats, flying drum kits and enough pyro to light up a small city, we're talking good old fashioned glam trash rock'n'roll !!! The '80s glam metal gods are laying 'em in the aisles all over the world….

"The entire event was a chance to let loose one's inner evil clown. There's little else that dares to be so brazen, so obvious, so obsessed with the pleasures of the moment" (Edmonton Sun)
"Big, loud and dirty" (MTV.com)
"The feel-good reunion of the year" (Entertainment Weekly)
"Evidently there is life after death. And it's a hell of a (freak) show" (NME)
"Pop and hair metal glory" (Beacon Journal)
"Wonderfully entertaining" (Ottawa Sun)
"One of the best heavy metal arena shows you'll likely see in this day and age" (Calgary Sun)
"An unqualified success" (Boston Herald)
"My rating - four devil horns" (Philadelphia Inquirer).

Get the picture – this tour is HOT!!!!

We all know the Mötley Crüe story. They built a monumental glam-metal following in their '80s LA heyday with a string of hit albums "Too Fast For Love", "Shout At The Devil", "Theatre Of Pain", "Girls Girls Girls" and "Dr Feelgood", and sold out stadiums to the tune of 10 million concert tickets. Yet all the forces that made Mötley Crüe's kick-ass music so authentic, namely their own reckless lifestyle of excess, gradually took its toll. In 1989 Nikki Sixx was revived after flatlining from a heroin overdose. Add to that brawls, lawsuits and just about every other shenanigan you can think of, and no wonder their official biography "The Dirt" is recognised by many as one of the best rock books ever written.

Fast forward six years and under the relentless persistence of a UK promoter, the band are back in the saddle. And, as one journalist noted, with the world gone crazy, what better time for a good-time shot in the arm of anthemic glam metal.

The band's "Red White And Crüe" album is now certified US platinum having sold more than a million copies, the band are soon to be presented with their own Hollywood Hall Of Fame star, a sensational double-live concert DVD from the tour titled "Carnival Of Sins" is about to hit the stores, and hell, everything is going so well the band are committed to recording a brand new studio album early next year!

Joining the Crüe on BLACKJACK will be their special Aussie tour guests MOTORHEAD. Lemmy Kilmister's passion for his band knows no bounds. "Motorhead is not only my job, it's my whole life". Celebrating 30 years since the release of their debut album "Ace Of Spades", Lemmy and the boys got the best reviews of their career for last year's fantastic "Inferno" album. This year they were awarded a Grammy for Best Metal Performance and are in rip-snorting form.

With a string of platinum albums to their name and one of the best live bands in the country THE LIVING END proudly step up to the plate at BLACKJACK. Doesn't matter whether you've seen them indoors or outdoors, club or stadium, THE LIVING END are the incendiary, fists-in-the-air singalong rock'n'roll guarantee.

And yes it's true. Melbourne' metal/ rock/ punk/ rockabilly gods THE FIREBALLS will officially reunite for this special occasion. The legend of the tattooed, mohawked, psychotic trio lives large, and with their entire back catalogue about to be re-released through a new on-line shop, the FIREBALLS are back in action.

Plus very special guests THE CASANOVAS & THE DAY OF THE DEAD.

THINGS YOU NEED TO KNOW:
CLAREMONT SHOWGROUNDS Main Arena. 5pm – 10pm. All General Admission, R+ 18 only. No BYO. No Passouts. We play rain or shine. Food and Beverage available. Entry via Station Plaza Gate at Showgrounds Train Station only.

Tickets: $99.99 includes bf & gst
TICKETS ON SALE FRIDAY AUGUST 19

Full Event Information and Online Bookings: www.heatseaker.com.au
Bookings: 136 100 and www.ticketmaster.com
Ticket Outlets: 78 Records (Perth), Mills Records (Fremantle), Beat Music (Karrinyup), Planet (Mt Lawley) and all Live clothing stores (Perth, Garden City, Claremont, Whitford City, Carousel, Karrinyup, Morley)

EVENT POLICY:
No BYO. No passouts. Food & beverage available on site. Both cheap bottled water and free tap water available on site. Hard containers and other potentially dangerous items will not be allowed into the event. This may include but is not limited to items such as large water containers, hard lunch boxes, thongs, pineapples, eskies, boats, spears, crocodiles, dangerous adornments, glass and other items deemed to be dangerous by event management and/or crowd control at their sole discretion. Absolutely no gang

colours, weapons, steel capped boots, aggro. Dress sensibly for weather conditions and an awesome rock show.

Proudly presented by Andrew McManus Presents and 96 FM.
www.heatseaker.com.au
www.motleycrue.com
www.ampresents.com

I came up with a concept for a new television show called On Tour With. I documented the proposed treatment for the series and got it in front of MTV, VH1 and Channel V in Australia to see if they had interest in it. Of course the first episode was ready to go – their camera crew could travel with me as I get to meet the band, see my first show and hang out on the road. Whilst they indicated they liked the concept, they eventually came back saying they had no budget for a new series. (I still think it's got merit as a music television series, so I might push it again one day.)

Towards the end of August, Nikki emailed me asking, "Are we going to eat 'gator again?" I told him, "It's called croc' down under" and said it would be good to go to a restaurant with him again, especially since last time he was feeling somewhat ill. I started thinking about all the other cool possibilities the tour could bring.

As the six promised dates drew closer, fans still held their hearts in their hands, hoping ticket sales were strong and the band's Australian tour would not get cancelled at the last minute as it did five years ago when the band was to tour down under behind their New Tattoo album. Everything was going ahead this time though.

September whizzed by and the publicist contacted me in October to see if I wanted to participate in a special promotion. To kickstart Crüe-fever, the promoter was to hold a special cinema screening of the Carnival of Sins DVD across the country. Tickets could only be won through radio MMM,

Channel V, Faster Louder, and my Chronological Crue website, where I offered diehard fans the chance of winning one of twenty double-tickets in each state. Everyone who was to attend would also be in the running for a chance to meet the band.

As the competition entries came in, I was now very keen to get my own tour plans organised. I got the itinerary through from band management in Los Angeles early in November and booked my flights. One of the flights listed was no longer showing as available by the airline, so I made some enquiries. It turned out that all the flights had in fact changed from the initial itinerary I had been sent, so I had to re-schedule my trip and pay more money if I wanted to be on the same flights as the band and therefore increase my chances of seeing them and spending time with them.

The Carnival of Sins DVD cinema-screening event then took place on Monday, November 14 at 7pm across Australia. I had a good chat with Melanie Holloway from Andrew McManus's office, after meeting her at the registration desk. We took our seats and let the excitement build. It was fantastic to see Mötley Crüe live in concert on the big cinema screen and hear the songs through their powerful sound system. The event certainly helped to create a buzz just a few weeks before the band were due to land in Australia, and fans enjoyed tasting the concert on the silver screen.

As the weeks and days inched closer to the tour, fans online were trying to make head and tail of the Fanfire package ticket situation. They were told they would have to pick up their tickets from Will Call at the venue on the day of the show and then fans started received tickets in the mail within the last week of the tour. Unfortunately, chaos ensued and many fans voiced their displeasure of the poor communication and customer service of Fanfire. For many fans, the tour did not get off to a good start.

I caught up with Nikki while he was in Japan, organising how we were going to catch up once he hit Australia. I offered to take him to Bon Scott's grave in Fremantle once we hit Perth and he was dead keen for me to take him there. "Hey Paul, Looking forward to seeing you.....we will have a blast. I'd love to go to Bon Scott's grave.....and any other stuff I should photograph."

Petrina rang me the day before the band arrived; stuck for ideas on what gifts they should give the band members from Universal Music Australia. Right off the bat I said I'm sure some nice bottles of Australian Pinot Grigio would go down great with Tommy Lee and Vince Neil. I suggested a pictorial coffee table book with great Australian landscape photographs for Nikki, since he'd been tripping out on photography lately. Mick Mars? Umm… that was a little more difficult. I was thinking along the lines of B-Grade horror and Sci-Fi but that didn't feel right. Petrina said, "He's got to eat right? So, how about a hamper or something?" Great idea. A gift basket hamper with Australian macadamia nuts and other assorted Australian treats. Cool. Let him get his own movies out and eat the food while he watches them.

Many friends and fans emailed me with all sorts of questions. "What hotel are they staying at?" "Sorry, I'm unable to give out any of the band's itinerary of course," was my reply. "Let's meet for a drink in Adelaide before the show." "Can you get me some tickets?" "I desperately need to meet them for five minutes, can you...?" Bottom line: I wouldn't make any promises, to any one, about anything.

When a show comes to town, and you want more action than just seeing the concert, it's a very unpredictable thing. There's only so much preparation that can be done; the rest you just have to roll with. Heck, I've also been waiting ages for my opportunities as well and I needed to put myself first for a change. I always like to help people out but I knew I needed to look after number one this time, first and foremost.

I sent an issue of my free Chronological Crue Newswire service to a thousand-plus subscribers all over the globe. It commenced with:

> Six years ago, I was honoured to be invited to write the liner notes in the first-ever Mötley Crüe live album – the double Live: Entertainment or Death CD. My piece summed up the band's live history from a fan's perspective. The great irony is that I was then – and still am now – yet to witness a live Mötley Crüe show! That is about to change this Saturday when I will see the band play the first of their six concerts across Australia. I will be traveling with the band to see all six shows as many dreams come true (so don't expect many updates to the site during this time). I will be capturing as much content as I can and documenting my tour adventures for you all to enjoy in some format once I have recovered, next year! In the meantime, read on to see what the Crüe has been up to this month.

I could feel myself getting very excited as I counted down the sleeps. I was glad I was extremely busy though, as being occupied kept me from dreaming all day about what lies ahead.

THE
JACK
AWARDS
2005
INVITATION

You are invited to:
THE 2005 JACK AWARDS
TUESDAY MAY 10, 2005
FROM 7.30PM SEYMOUR CENTRE
CNR CLEVELAND ST & CITY RD CHIPPENDALE NSW
LIVE PERFORMANCES BY:
THE LIVING END
SPIDERBAIT
ESKIMO JOE
THE COPS
SPECIAL PERFORMANCE
BY AN ALL STAR JAM
HOSTED BY JABBA
BLACK CARPET AND COCKTAILS 7.30PM-8.45PM
AWARDS CEREMONY 9PM-10.20PM
RSVP ESSENTIAL:
This invitation is for yourself only.
Wrist bands must be worn to gain access. Seats are limited.

MÖTLEY
CRÜE
RED, WHITE AND CRUE TOUR 2005
with very
SPECIAL GUESTS
motörhead
MÖTLEY
CRÜE
Sat 3 Dec - SYDNEY Superdome
Tues 6 Dec - MELBOURNE Vodafone Arena

Andrew McManus & Triple M present
MÖTLEY CRÜE
RED WHITE & CRUE TOUR
motörhead
THE CASANOVAS
TUE 6th DEC
Melbourne
VODAFONE
ARENA
Ticketek 132 849
RCP

ARRY
ROCK CLUB

Friday, December 2, 2005 - Melbourne

Having arrived from Japan on Tuesday with the crew, Mick Mars was now joined in Sydney by Nikki Sixx following his trip to Cambodia and Thailand, Tommy Lee from his holiday in Bali, and Vince Neil who had been catching plenty of the harsh Australian sun at Surfer's Paradise on Queensland's famous Gold Coast.

Word had come through from the record company a few days prior that a press conference was to take place in Sydney at 1pm today. I had always planned to arrive in Sydney from Melbourne on the day of the first show, Sat 3rd, as I wanted my family to all be together to celebrate my son's fifteenth birthday today. So I organised for my friend Brendan Thomson, or Dr. Shinbone Starr as he likes to be called for some reason, to attend the press conference to cover it on behalf of Chronological Crue, since he had arrived in Sydney on Wednesday.

Shinbone made his way to the InterContinental hotel and up to the Premier's Room on level two. He set up his video camera on a tripod and captured the afternoon's events.

The press conference was hosted by Richard Wilkins, currently the entertainment reporter on Channel Nine's national morning TV show, Today. The former host of MTV during its six-year run on Australian television is now said to be one of the most successful and popular entertainment personalities in Australia.

Here is a blow-by-blow transcript of Mötley Crüe's Australian press conference:

HOST: Ladies and gentlemen. On behalf of Andrew McManus Presents and Universal Music, it is my great pleasure to welcome you here today to our press conference with Mötley Crüe. Now, the boys start their eagerly awaited Australian tour tomorrow night at the Sydney SuperDome before heading off around the country. It's been an amazing year for them as I'm sure you're aware. They've just arrived here from Japan and have been on the road pretty much full-time for most of this year. If you are unfamiliar with this, there's a little pack here for you with the Carnival of Sins Mötley Crüe DVD. This is kind of what we're going to see on stage, but to tell us all about it, would you please welcome, the four members of Mötley Crüe: Mick Mars, Nikki Sixx, Tommy Lee and Vince Neil. Ladies and gentlemen, put your hands together for Mötley Crüe!

(The band walks out into the room, one behind the other, to loud applause before standing together as press photographers flash away. After a minute of two, Nikki says, "Alright that's it" and they move to take their seats; Tommy on the left, then Mick, Vince and Nikki on the far right.)

HOST: Welcome gentlemen, nice to have you here.

NIKKI: Thank you very much.

HOST: Great to see the four of you again. This has been a pretty amazing run for you since you decided to get back together. About twelve months ago you were in rehearsals if I recall.

NIKKI: Something like that. That's where we met then.

HOST: It's been amazing since then. The tour's gone off. It's been full on.

TOMMY: It has been amazing actually. Yeh, it's been amazing.

HOST: Well, we have the cream of the Australian media here, assembled for you today. Ladies and gentlemen, questions from the floor?

MICK: WHAT?

(The audience doesn't quite know what to make of Mick's sudden, loud outburst. Tommy sips from his glass of red wine on the desk)

MEDIA: It's now been fifteen years since you played here guys. Can you remember any of it – the last time?

TOMMY: No.

(Audience laughter)

VINCE: Is it that long is it? Wow!

TOMMY: '89… '90?

MEDIA: '90.

VINCE: Wow.

TOMMY: I remember the Gold Coast.

VINCE: Well, the funny thing is I just came from the Gold Coast. I just stayed at the same hotel that we were at fifteen years ago… at the same bar.

MEDIA: Are you guys still pinching yourself that you're out playing massive areas… (Inaudible)

NIKKI: What was the question?

MEDIA: Are you pinching yourself that you're back playing arenas all over the place to 20,000 people a night?

NIKKI: Can we 'what' ourselves?

(Audience laughter)

MEDIA: Are you still pinching yourselves to be back…

NIKKI: Picturing ourselves?

VINCE: Pinching. (He motions to pinch Nikki on the ass)

NIKKI: Oh, pinching!

(Audience laughter)

NIKKI: If you pinch, please pinch in the front.

VINCE: Ooooo.

NIKKI: I think we're grateful to get to do what we like to do and that people still care. It feels good, yeh.

VINCE: We're just happy that the fans are out and they want to see the band. Whether it's small places… when we started this whole thing, we didn't say 'OK, well we'll only be happy if it's arenas' and stuff. You know, it just happened and we're grateful, obviously. The fans are there so it's been a lot of fun.

(Nikki lights up a smoke)

MEDIA: How much of your popularity now do you think is nostalgic?

TOMMY: It's kind of weird. Like, for the first time in our careers, we look around at the audience and it's so cool to see that this whole new generation of people are out. Like, we meet people every day backstage; one of the youngest kids I saw at the show was sitting in the front row. His father brought him. He's like nine years old and he's up there going like "Yeeeaaahhhh" (holds his hands up with the metal horns). And I was like, 'man!' So every day now, which it hasn't been like that for a while, this whole new generation is coming to see us now. You see like nine-year-olds to forty-five-year-olds, so it's really cool.

VINCE: It's not just the folks coming to see us.

TOMMY: The old punks. (Said in an English accent)

VINCE: (laughs) But yeh, it's really cool. Like Tommy was saying, we've been doing these Meet and Greets before the show and like, there'll be a family and they'll be bringing their kids to their very first rock concert – and it would be us! So you see twelve, thirteen, or fourteen-year-olds with Shout At The Devil shirts on, which they weren't even born when that came out.

TOMMY: (laughs) Yeh, sitting on their parent's shoulders, you know. Cool.

MEDIA: You guys have your own tour buses when you're touring the States and that. Do you guys still find time to hang out?

NIKKI: We try not to hang out though. (Smirks)

(Audience laughter)

TOMMY: We still try.

VINCE: Yeh, where did we all just come from?

TOMMY: Yeh.

NIKKI: We were in four different parts of the country. Usually when we do interviews we have a wall between us, but we're trying to… we've had a therapist on the road with us, trying to help us. (Laughing)

VINCE: They're still working on it. (Motioning to the lack of wall between him and Nikki) Well you know what we try to do is what we've learnt in the twenty-five years that we've been touring is to make ourselves comfortable. And we're in a position where we can be comfortable and a lot of the press is… when people said that was because we don't get along, we don't this and this… but it was because it makes us comfortable. And if you can afford it you can do it, you know. Tommy has his kids come out and Nikki has his kids come out… and I have my dogs come out.

(Audience laughter)

TOMMY: Can you imagine all that with everybody's families on one bus? It'd be like 'Arrrggghhh!'

VINCE: That'd be crazy.

NIKKI: I just went to see the Eagles in Los Angeles before I came here and they all have separate dressing rooms and they travel separately and I asked Timothy [Schmit], the bass player… I said, "Does the press always ask you if you guys like hate each other because you travel separately?" He goes, "Isn't that stupid?" I said, "Yeh, well I guess it seems like that's what it would be but it really isn't that at all."

VINCE: A lot of people still think we still live in the same house together.

(Audience laughter)

NIKKI: That would be killer!

(Audience laughter – Vince's security guy Ray brings Vince a glass of white wine)

TOMMY: We just played a couple of shows with The Rolling Stones, which was fucking awesome, and those guys: Keith and Ronnie… Mick traveling on his own…

NIKKI: They had their own dressing rooms.

TOMMY: They always had their own space, you know. They get together and do what they do best.

NIKKI: And we don't live together. That's a good point.

TOMMY: We lived together long enough.

NIKKI: Yeh, exactly.

VINCE: Yeh.

NIKKI: We paid our dues.

MEDIA: Tommy, you don't look like the discipline type. What was it like starring in Tommy Lee Goes to College?

TOMMY: It was fun. Like, I was seventeen years old when we got a recording contract and we've been making records and touring ever since, so I bailed on my… I had like two months to go on my senior year of high school, so I never had the opportunity to go to college. So when I got approached to do this, at first I was like 'Oh, I don't know' and then I thought about it and I thought this might be kind of fun to get a little taste of one semester of college and go make a really funny TV show and see if I could actually pull it off. So it was cool; it was a challenge.

VINCE: And he learnt. (Laughs)

TOMMY: Yep and I also learnt, made some good friends, and had lots of sex.

(Audience laughter)

MEDIA: Guys, will we see a new album in 2006?

TOMMY: I'm sorry?

MEDIA: Will we see a new album in 2006?

TOMMY: Yeh. We're touring until April – the beginning of April – and then I'm sure we'll take a little time off and then we'll start writing and making some new racket. Yeh.

MEDIA: I'm led to believe that the new DVD features a tittie cam. Can you explain what this might be?

TOMMY: A tittie cam? It's pretty self-explanatory.

(Audience laughter)

VINCE: Very.

TOMMY: Fun for the whole family.

VINCE: Well I was actually in the Hard Rock [Café] in Tokyo and they were playing the whole…

TOMMY: DVD.

VINCE: Yeh, the DVD, and it came to the tittie cam and it was like (Vince motions a cut across his neck with his hand) blink – off! There's a lot of little kids in the Hard Rock.

MEDIA: Guys, why have you lasted so long when your contemporaries, or your musical peers, didn't last?

TOMMY: What was that?

NIKKI: I think that there's a few of us that came out around the same time: U2, Metallica, and us. There's a lot of bands; it's stiff competition out there and I think, for us there's something unique about us, you know. Whether it's the way Vince sings, or Mick plays guitar, it just separates us just enough. So long as we stay together, we can continue down that path making new music.

MEDIA: You've had some line-up changes in the past. Did you realise that this was the only Mötley Crüe? (The band members all look at each other and laugh)

(Audience laughter)

VINCE: Well, there's been different versions of Mötley Crüe throughout the years you know. Like when Tommy was gone, we had other drummers – it wasn't Mötley Crüe. And when I was gone and these guys were playing – it wasn't Mötley Crüe. And when I was singing and doing Mötley Crüe songs in solo bands – it's not Mötley Crüe. Mötley Crüe is the four of us and it always has been. Like Tommy was saying, he was seventeen when we got the contract. I was eighteen. We went to high school together you know… just growing up and being together and you can't just replace people.

NIKKI: Except for Mick. (Nikki throws a scrunched piece of paper that hits Mick's hat and bounces next to Tommy)

(Audience laughter)

MICK: I'll kill you.

TOMMY: (He picks the paper ball up) Give me goal posts. (Vince and Nikki hold their hands apart and Tommy flicks the paper off the desk and it just drops short of Vince's hands) Ooooh!

MEDIA: Mick, your health's been well documented…

MICK: I'm sorry?

MEDIA: Your health has been well documented. How much of a struggle is it to keep up with the massive schedule and get out on stage and perform for two hours every night? Well, not every night – every second night?

MICK: Well, let me see. (He points to Vince) He was in a wheelchair for a while because he pulled a leg muscle. (He points to Tommy) And he got blown up…

(Audience laughter)

MICK: …and I'm still walking. So what does that tell you?

TOMMY: Nikki got caught on fire.

VINCE: Yeh, he got caught on fire too. (They all point to Nikki)

NIKKI: Oh yeh; I try to get out of that one.

MICK: He got caught on fire but I'm all good.

TOMMY: So far, so good; Mick has been the only one unscathed.

VINCE: And Mick… you know, throughout all the years, this is like one of the only tours where actually Mick's getting in my way. You know, I try and run back and forth on stage and you're everywhere – Mick's everywhere now. You know, he's…

MICK: I'm like a snail.

(Audience laughter)

VINCE: Mick is playing better, moving better, rocking better than he ever has in his whole life.

NIKKI: Yeh.

TOMMY: Yeh.

VINCE: And I'm proud of him for that.

MICK: Thank you.

MEDIA: Guys, the book *The Dirt* was an amazing read and we've heard rumours of a possible film of the book. Who is going to portray each of you in this film and how developed is the project?

VINCE: Just a bunch of old guys I guess.

(Audience laughter)

MICK: They can't all be old guys – except for me.

VINCE: That's right; you started out as an old guy.

MICK: That's right.

VINCE: Well, we haven't got to the casting point yet. Paramount Pictures and MTV Films have combined forces in making the film and we've read the script, we've made changes to the script, so now it's gone through to the director phase. Making movies is very, very time consuming. If it comes out, it comes out. Hopefully… (He turns his head towards Nikki) Will we even have a say in who plays us?

NIKKI: Yeh, absolutely.

VINCE: Cool. (Laughs)

NIKKI: I hope.

MICK: I'm gonna play Tom Werman. (They all laugh) Chicken! It makes sense.

VINCE: To us. (Laughing) Chicken.

NIKKI: We have our little inside language.

MICK: They're trying to save me but just didn't get it. FUCKING NUTS!

(Audience laughter)

MEDIA: You guys are playing with Motörhead tomorrow. Are you guys fans of those guys?

VINCE: I'm sorry?

MEDIA: You're playing with Motörhead…

VINCE: Oh, Motörhead?

TOMMY: Motörhead.

VINCE: I didn't find out until this morning.

(Audience laughter)

VINCE: That's pretty bad. I didn't know who was playing with us.

NIKKI: Vince checks his emails like a year later.

VINCE: I'll check 'em when we get back to the States.

NIKKI: Yeh.

VINCE: That's gonna be cool though.

TOMMY: Yeh it's awesome.

VINCE: I think it's great. I'm excited. I'm a fan, so I'll be out there watching... Lemmy.

HOST: A couple more questions?

MEDIA: Guys, Australian fan Paul Miles has been running the Chronological Crue website for over a decade now. How important do you guys feel it's been in making people aware of the band's history and getting you back to Australia today?

NIKKI: Chronological Crue – well, I talk to different people from MTV and VH1 and that seems to be a real go-to spot for information on the band – more so than our own website.

TOMMY: Paul knows more about us than we know. (Laughs)

NIKKI: That's very true.

TOMMY: It gets kind of scary.

NIKKI: Yeh, I've read it before and gone 'We did that?'

(Audience laughter)

TOMMY: He's a stalker.

(Mick whispers to Tommy, "Who?")

TOMMY: Paul Miles, the Chronological Crue guy.

MICK: Oh.

TOMMY: He's a stalker.

(Audience laughter)

TOMMY: Just kidding.

MEDIA: Guys, do you get any time to do any sightseeing? Opera House, cuddle the koalas… any time-off to see any of the sights around Sydney?

VINCE: Actually, we all just got here today, except for Mick. Mick's been here for like five days. Tommy was in Bali and Nikki was in Bangkok and I was in Surfers [Paradise] and we all just got here.

TOMMY: Yeh.

VINCE: Mick, did you do sightseeing?

MICK: Yeh, right out my window.

(Audience laughter)

TOMMY: The Foo Fighters are playing tonight. I'm gonna go check them out.

NIKKI: Oh that's cool.

TOMMY: And then who knows from there.

MEDIA: How different is the set-list every night? Are you sort of chopping and changing…

TOMMY: How do we finish the what?

MEDIA: How different is the set-list every night? Are you chopping and changing from throughout your career?

TOMMY: Well, this set-list is probably the most extensive that we've ever played. I mean, we play… See, it's like two hours and fifteen minutes or so. We play stuff we've never played before ever, from the very beginning of our career right up to the new stuff on Red, White & Crüe. So we play a shit-load of songs.

VINCE: We can't really change them, you know, like from day to day just because everything nowadays is so computerised…

TOMMY: Lighting, pyro.

VINCE: …Pyro cues, so this set-list basically stays the same.

HOST: Final question?

MEDIA: You guys picked up the journalist Neil Strauss for writing *The Dirt*. Recently Neil Strauss wrote his book *The Game*, which is about his experience as a pick-up artist. Did you guys give him any tips, and if so, can you share some of them for our readers? (The band members all look at each other, perplexed.)

TOMMY: Any tips for my readers? What, what?

MEDIA: You know Neil Strauss? You know you spent time with Neil.

TOMMY: Yes.

MEDIA: He's a pick-up artist now and you must have had some sort of influence on him…

VINCE: He's a pick-up artist?

MEDIA: Well he claims to be.

(Audience laughter)

VINCE: So he's pimping out now?

TOMMY: Well, the last time I saw him he'd just finished that book and he was hanging out with Jenna Jameson, so he must be doing alright – hanging out with porn stars. But then again, he wrote her book didn't he?

NIKKI: That's right. So maybe he knew it was kind of working for him.

MEDIA: So you don't have any tips?

TOMMY: From Neil?

MEDIA: No, to give to Neil.

MICK: Wear protection!

(Audience laughter)

HOST: OK, is there a question to follow that one, ladies and gents? (Silence) Final question? (Silence) I think that's it gentlemen; I think you've satisfied the Australian media. We welcomed you here today. Thank you for coming. Thank you for facing the media. Enjoy your stay. Have a good time.

(The audience applauses loudly as the band stands and photographers move in to snap them all standing together again, before they exit the room with their minders)

So with the twenty-minute press conference now over, I received a few photos of the event in my email from Universal Records later that afternoon. I added a couple of these to the Chronological Crue website, as perhaps some proof to Australian fans that the four original members of Mötley Crüe were finally together again in our country after fifteen years, and ready to rock us over the next week.

My family and I then enjoyed the birthday celebrations, dining at my son's choice of restaurant – Japanese. After one final check of my email when we got home, it was time for that last sleep. However, I don't think I got much sleep, thinking about all that was to lie ahead with the Mötley tour and my opportunity to finally see them live in concert after all these years. My hand-luggage bag was packed and I was ready to set off on my adventures – but I had to wait for morning first.

THE BAND YOU NEVER THOUGHT YOU'D SEE LIVE AGAIN ARE HERE!
MÖTLEY CRÜE
Mötley Crüe Press Conference
Friday December 2nd @ 1pm
Intercontinental Hotel
Premier's Room Level 2
117 Macquarie St, Sydney
Room access from 12.30pm
Please RSVP to Chrissie Camp
telephone 02 [redacted]
chrissie@[redacted].com.au

MÖTLEY CRÜE RED, WHITE & CRUE
AUSTRALIAN TOUR - 2005

WHITEBOY

Saturday, December 3, 2005 - Melbourne to Sydney

As my eyes opened, I realised there was zero sleeps to go – the countdown had finally come to a close. I tediously chewed through some Vegemite on toast before my wife Sara [pronounced Sarah] took me on the ten-minute drive to the city bus stop. After a long kiss goodbye, I got on board the bus and stared across the passing views as we ventured north up the freeway to Melbourne's Tullamarine airport, thinking thorough all the possible scenarios that I may encounter on tour, with an eagerness to ensure I maximised every opportunity that came my way or that I could possibly create. My long-awaited rock'n'roll adventure was underway as I was now moving further outside familiar territory.

Arriving at the airport, I checked in to get my boarding pass and walked towards the designated boarding gate. I had time on my side and took opportunity to stop by the bar/café. As I ordered a latte, I noticed a group of men further inside swigging beers with a combination of smiles and blank looks on their faces. They looked like musicians; they looked English, and upon further inquisitive looks; I spotted one of the Gallaghers. Sure enough, it was the lads from Oasis and their touring party.

As I sipped my hot coffee, I kept glancing towards them every so often, knowing that their Australian tour was in full swing, as mine was just beginning. As I looked at each member of their touring party, I wondered what role they performed in bringing the concert to their fans. I listened across to conversations as much as I could, trying to catch words of any rock'n'roll stories. A small group of autograph hunters stood in the main corridor, waiting for their opportunity to pounce and capture a memory and story to be told to their friends. It built my anticipation even more.

I finished my coffee, and headed further towards my boarding gate. On the way, I passed a sharp-dressed man with a beautiful Asian-looking woman holding a cute little boy. They caught my eye. The man's face was familiar; I thought he looked similar to Perry Farrell from the band Jane's Addiction. I shook my head and told myself to get a grip. If I was to be spending a week on the road, I couldn't be thinking everyone I saw was a rockstar.

The flight was good – really good. I was as ready as I was ever going to be. I had prepared fully and was enjoying the day, as I knew it would be the day that I finally got to see Mötley Crüe live; a date that I would probably remember forever: 3rd Dec 2005. Landing in Sydney, I walked hastily to the underground train station as the quickest/best value way to get me into the city. I got off at Central Station and following the small map in my hand, I walked to my hotel destination in Ultimo.

I soon arrived at the Mercure hotel having worked up a small sweat in the warmer Sydney sunshine. I made my way up to the hotel room of my Melbourne friends Eric Chow and Mel Felekidis, who were gracious enough to let me crash with them for the night. Expecting a foldout couch, I was pleasantly surprised with a single bed to come back to once my momentous occasion was over. Thanks guys!

With the afternoon fast ticking away and an eagerness to get to the venue as soon as possible, we quickly arranged to meet up with other friends back at Central Station en route to the SuperDome in Homebush; site of the 2000 Sydney Olympics. Homework told us that the train was the best way to make the journey. We met friends from Brisbane and Melbourne on Platform 18 and we were soon on the next Lidcombe-bound train, sharing stories of our travels to date. The connecting Olympic Park sprint train took us into the heart of the large Olympic village and amongst many other fans making their way to the show.

As we strolled between foreign buildings and across parklands, I took opportunity to phone my mum and wish her a happy birthday. She was surprised to hear from me since she knew it was to be a busy, special day for me in another state. I'm glad I made the time to make her enjoy her day more, before I got swept away with the night and its imminent celebrations.

After a short walk, we found ourselves outside the venue and were soon looking for the ticket windows. We joined the short queue and I asked the staff member behind the glass to check for tickets under the surname Miles. No go. "Please check again," I said. I watched her check through various folders and plastic boxes of envelopes with alphabetical dividers; still no such luck. After explaining how my tickets had been organised, she advised that 'promoter tickets' were still being prepared and wouldn't be ready until 6pm. The nerves set in.

Other people came and went with tickets in hand. We stood looking through the glass perimeter of the foyer as fans increasingly passed their tickets through the scanners, entered the arena and started to buy merchandise and drink beers. As 6pm passed, I asked a couple more times about ticket readiness, only to be told they are still being prepared. With no idea of whether my tickets and passes would finally arrive, I took some heart after seeing the familiar face of Sammy Dalton stuffing envelopes with tickets in a back room, even though the hard riffs of support band The Casanovas could now be heard emanating from the auditorium.

Hanging around the ticket window, waiting, online friends in Andrew Treadwell and Tim James crossed my path. Whilst it was good to have a yak with these guys, my mind was focused on the hope of everything working out with my tickets. Petrina from Universal Music soon came along. It was good to catch up with Petrina again, who was meeting other industry people for a Meet and Greet with the band. Damn – I hate waiting for tickets. Memories of being stood up at the ticket window for an Alice Cooper concert and heading home without seeing the show after exhausting all possible ways of resolving the situation came flooding back.

Thankfully, a new ticket window opened and the call was put out that promoter tickets were now ready. I opened my envelope and the sight of an All Access pass filled my eyes.

YES! The wait was worth it; Jeff Varner's promise was good. Shinbone and I then looked at our tickets and compared where we were both seated. Sammy was kind enough to swap some tickets around so we had seats next to each other.

With a smile on our faces, we headed to the front entrance, observing security patting down everyone's pants and checking inside bags. I took my digital camera out of my jeans pocket and put in down the front of my underpants before joining the queue. After making it into the foyer without hassle, we bumped into other friends from the train and told them briefly of our nervous wait as they lined up for beers.

With time ticking by, we decided to quickly suss out how to get backstage to try and meet up with Nikki Sixx. An usher pointed us in the direction of the elevator to go down to the backstage area. In the lift, our passes were checked and it was explained that my All Access pass was required to 'escort' the two VIP passes of Shinbone and his friend Slav.

Out of the elevator, we walked around designated areas of equipment storage, road crew going about their business and the investigative eyes of staff trying to sight our required passes. Another flash of my pass and we were heading down a backstage corridor with rooms off to each side. Looking in the rooms as I passed the doorways, my eyes soon caught an approaching tattooed figure with big black hair straight ahead. Sixx!

He said something, we said something – I can't remember what; time blurred. It seemed he recognised the bald-headed Shinbone at once, perhaps after having spotted him at yesterday's press conference. He took longer to recognise me with longer, darker hair than the first and only time we last met fifteen months ago. A hug later, he took us through to his dressing room where we sat around and re-acquainted amongst the pleasantly incense-scented room. Nikki introduced us to his security guard Kimo (Carlson Silva); a huge Hawaiian chap with cropped hair that looked like he could make a real mess of you if you did him or Nikki wrong.

I wasn't the only one who had changed appearance in the last year though. I couldn't believe how much slimmer and fitter Nikki looked, initially putting it down to him being so busy on stage most nights this year as the difference. As we sat in his dressing room, I complimented him, saying he looking in great shape. "Fit for Life," he said. I looked at some plastic bottles of nutritional items in front of me. He certainly looked fit. Without prying any further, I made a mental note of the three-word phrase and looked it up later. Harvey Diamond was the guy who introduced his Fit for Life philosophy of meal-mixing tips for weight loss. Twelve million of his books have now been sold, after an initial forty weeks on The New York Times Best Seller List in the mid-'80s.

Sixx had his laptop setup on the coffee table draped with leopard print material and was immediately full of stories of his recent Cambodia and Thailand trip. "Here, check this out!" We huddled around the screen of his Mac as he displayed photo after photo from his trip and told us the stories behind each. 'This little boy was so pleased that he found a fish, he put it in a jar to take home and keep. The fish was floating on top of the water in the jar, but he was still very pleased.' The clarity and quality of the pictures and their subjects were certainly impressive. 'Look at this one with the railway tracks running right through. There are SO many people that live here in these slums.' Heavy.

'Check out the breasts! We paid a small amount of money to enter a he-she bar and do whatever we wanted. They thought I was strange when I said all I want to do is take some photographs. Isn't he amazing?' Sixx was then telling us the population size of Cambodia, and how they are ridiculously outnumbered by the amount of live landmines that frequently explode as they (and their cows) go about their daily lives. Heavy, heavy metal. Then came photos of victims with body parts missing and his tales of the cash they passed out against local advice. Somehow, witnessing my first Mötley Crüe show was now the last thing running through my mind.

Having not had dinner, I was eyeing off a deli tray still wrapped in plastic that sat invitingly on a bench. I asked Sixx if I could have a pick and he said sure, and said I could go to catering and get a real feed if I wanted. I declined the catering, as I maneuvered large slices of deli meats into my mouth, not really wanting to leave the room and miss any of the experience.

Nikki said he struggled at yesterday's press conference. Having shown us photos of what he had just been experiencing, he said he was then faced with flashing cameras in his face that disorientated him to some degree. Then he was faced with questions about whether all four guys get along with each other and he's thinking of limbless people that are trying to get on with their lives. We could appreciate what he was saying and the culture shock he must have been feeling.

Time ticked by and Nikki soon said he'd better get ready for the show. Saying goodbye to him and Kimo until we were to meet up again after the show, we wandered out of his dressing room and into the hall, hoping to meet up with other band members. Mick Mars was the only one in sight, standing outside his dressing room now ready to rock. We introduced ourselves to him, along with his huge minder nicknamed Rhyno (Chris Eickstaed) and his nurse Tam by his side. Mick was already in joking mood and proceeded to make us laugh – just what we needed to reset the mood after Nikki's disturbing tales and imagery.

As conversation moved into technicalities of guitar setup, I wandered off down the hall to have a look in a few more rooms for something more stimulating. I saw one of the Crüe's dancers sorting through a pile of boots with a wardrobe lady, so I introduced myself; she was Alecia Schultze. The eyes on the dancer's pretty face were engaging and she seemed interested as to why I was backstage. I explained and told Alecia that I would be doing all six shows of the Australian tour. I also said that I have some friends that would like to meet up with her again; having met in Las Vegas with a promise to show her the sights of Brisbane once the tour arrived. She showed me her brand new tattoo on the waistline of her right hip. Nice ink.

I soon headed out into the corridor again towards my friends, before we were told we had to clear out of the backstage area now as everyone needed to get ready for the show. This felt a little odd considering I had an All Access pass, so I put it down to 'three's a crowd'. Motörhead had finished their set so it was time to get ready in position to see the Crüe show anyway.

We headed upstairs to the refreshments areas and entry doors. I was keen to get a scotch or beer but the lines of alcohol-seekers were ridiculously long and I didn't want to miss the start of the Mötley show. A bucket of chips and a Coke seemed a more sensible option. Refreshments in hand, we made our way to our ticketed seats with ten minutes until show time. As I sat halfway up the side of the arena and looked at all the people, a strange feeling came over me. I was buzzing that the show was about to start and I was about to see the Crüe live on stage for the first time, but at the same time I felt I wanted to be closer; I wanted to be amongst the action more and felt my seats were not going to be an ideal first experience.

I then realised I had an All Access pass that would probably allow me to wander down into the floor area where I knew a mate Adam Hodges from Newcastle was sitting with friends in seats 1, 2, 3 and 4 of Row 10. I thought I'd go and say hello to him while waiting for the show to start. I walked past an usher and onto the floor area, taking the shortest route to his seat location – through the walkway between the front row and the barricade. As I walked through with my eyes scanning about ten rows back for his face, I heard a couple of people call my name and tap me.

Looking down, I saw it was my friend Corrie Barrett from Melbourne and friend Dave Adams from Adelaide – next to each other. I don't think they knew each other. So I stopped, squatted to their level and had a chat with them… about something. In an instant the sounds of the AC/DC house music faded along with the house lights. I was faced with darkness and the screams of fans as they made their way towards me and the front of the stage. I turned around and took up position on the front barricade with Dave and Corrie, dead-set front and centre. Holy shit! I didn't really realise the enormity of what had just happened. I was actually on my way to see Adam in row 10 and now I was front row – front fucking row!

The tension built inside me as Mighty Mike jumped around the stage, revving the crowd up, before Alecia contorted and caressed with fellow dancer Brandy Wirtz in ways I knew she would be capable of. The glow of flame pots could be seen through the curtain as the opening bars of Shout At The Devil '97 filled my ears and heart. The first time this version of the classic was heard was at the American Music Awards on 27th January 1997 – the night Vince Neil reunited with the Crüe at the American Music Awards and the day my Chronological Crue website was launched for Crüeheads worldwide to enjoy. It was now the first song I was to witness the Crüe perform live – right in front of me!

As others jumped, thrust and pumped the air around me, my only movements were those from the bumps and force of others, as I stood still and let all my senses take in as much as possible, determined not to spill a drop of emotion. Wow! What an opening. It was everything I had hoped it would be. As the band progressed through Too Fast For Love and Ten Seconds To Love, I loosened up somewhat and began to rock along with the boys some more. Nikki soon noticed me in the front row and gave me a nod and a big smile, pleased to see me in pole position.

At the end of Ten Seconds, the stage filled with darkness and soon a solitary spotlight shone on Nikki Sixx as he approached his microphone. He stood tall and still, waiting, letting the noise from the crowd build. "Long time no see motherfuckers," started his welcoming introduction. "We want to dedicate this song… to Mr. Paul Miles. This song is called… Red fucking Hot!" and I was soon being bumped, elbowed and patted by on the head by people around who knew who I was.

It's hard to describe the wave of emotions that then flowed through my body. I was so proud, so pleased, so shocked, and so surprised. My mind started reflecting on how long I had been waiting for this time that I finally got to see the Crüe play live. I thought about the work I had dedicated to Mötley activities each and every day over the last decade for the love of the band. I thought about what they meant to me, what this moment meant to me and what I just heard, and it just poured out. I stood in still disbelief with a constant stream of tears rolling down my cheeks. My only movement was when I mouthed "thank you" to Sixx as he moved to centre stage and made eye contact again. He smiled with that big Sixx grin. Whatever happened from that moment on would be cream. If I died tomorrow, I would be a satisfied man. With wipes of my eyes, I took advice from the next song On With The Show and enjoyed the other old classics that followed into intermission.

As I was watching Tommy Lee, some songs after the short break, I saw him throw a drumstick towards the crowd. I managed to keep sight of it as it passed through the smoke and lights of the stage. I caught it in the air with a hand on each end of the stick. As I brought it down, another guy's hand got a solid grip in between mine before a flurry of vicious late hands tried to get a grip. Shaking them off, I tugged firmly with both my hands, only to be tugged back by the guy with a grip in the middle of the stick. With his free hand, he started flicking my All Access laminate, asking if I was a Platinum ticket-holder because he was. As he tried to pull rank over me, I let go of the stick and told him to enjoy it. He was still intent on showing me how much of a fan he was with his Crüe tattoos and how he deserved it more, but I wasn't about to enter his competition.

As I took up my position at the barricade again I felt my hand was sticky and sore. Inspecting it in the available stage lighting, I saw I had a few deep cuts on my right hand from the fingernails of those scrambling for the stick. Highlights from the Dr. Feelgood album came and went before Tommy came to front of stage to take hold of the Tittie Cam. What I saw made me think back to someone's earlier remark that it's always the roughest of chicks with the ugliest of boobs that are first to display. The Sydney crowd didn't seem as forthcoming as

Tommy expected, and to me he came off as too desperate and harassing, to the detriment of the show. Overall though, I think the band had to work quite hard to draw response from the seventy-seven percent capacity Sydney crowd of 9,216 than I had anticipated.

My favourite song Kickstart My Heart was up next to restore the appropriate mood. This was followed by a "thank you, goodnight" from Vince as the band exited and prepared for the encore of Anarchy In The U.K. The circus was in full swing for the finale with Mighty Mike riding his unicycle and swallowing fire. Next-to-nude dancers breathed and danced with fire, while another jumped around the stage on stilts to the beat of the anthem. As I watched Nikki Sixx move in front of me centre stage, my reaction was too slow to avoid his spray of blood into my face. It dripped down onto my neck and arm. I ducked when Tommy and Nikki grabbed a plastic bucket full of blood each to empty onto the bodies in the first few rows and thankfully the liquid covered those to either side of me instead this time.

The house lights soon came on and the show was over. I couldn't believe it. I said goodbyes to Corrie and Dave before spotting Shinbone and Slav in their seats halfway up the side of the area. As I approached them, they realised I had been up front when they saw the blood covering my face. I then saw Petrina from Universal in the same section and we were both spinning out again at Nikki's song dedication; she knew what these shows meant to me. We then headed outside to meet up with Eric and Mel and arrange to meet them later, probably at Iguana Bar in Kings Cross. I bumped into numerous other friends and found myself rushing to head backstage again.

We ventured down the corridor again and Kimo let us in to Nikki's dressing room where talk centered on the show and our thoughts of it. Nikki laughed at my blood-splattered face and said he was trying to remember where I was so he could avoid me – nice try Sixx!

We talked about the widely used Australian chant mainly used at sporting events: "Aussie, Aussie, Aussie; Oi, Oi, Oi."

Nikki was keen to try it at the next Crüe show but was nervous of the response he may get. We encouraged him with confidence to give it a shot, knowing he would get a great response back from the crowd. He said it would be on our heads if he didn't. It took him a while to get it right. "No Sixx, it's not Ussie, Ussie, Ussie, it's Ozzy, Ozzy, Ozzy!"

At one point during conversation, Nikki said they had done like 170 shows this tour and whilst it was great, they were really looking forward to their break coming up soon. I remarked that tonight was actually show number 134 for this year. Nikki just laughed and said, "Well YOU would fucking know!"

I asked Nikki whatever came of the song Future Ex-Wife that he been writing that day that we last went out for dinner in Melbourne. He thought for a minute and said that it actually became Sick Love Song. Cool. I said he could perhaps mention something along those lines before they play it live in Melbourne and he said that was a good idea (although he forgot to in the end).

As I sat on the couch next to Nikki, Shinbone snapped a photo of us in our blue jeans and black tops before I got up and returned favour for him and Slav. I grabbed a Powerade from his drinks rider tub and as time passed, we said we'd catch up with him tomorrow in Shinbone's hometown of Brisbane and we headed back outside the arena.

The majority of the crowd had dispersed and there wasn't a taxi in sight. We took the short walk back to the train station and caught the last bus into Lidcombe but found ourselves without a connecting train back into the city. With still no taxis in sight, we waited an hour or so for the Nightrider bus, recounting tales of the day and looking forward to more ahead. Even though we had every intent on having some drinks in Kings Cross, the long bus ride has quelled our desire and we decided to walk back to our various hotels from the last bus stop at the Town Hall instead.

Hungry, I stopped in at KFC. I felt the wary eyes of many young people cautiously sizing me up as I ate my Zinger burger. Thinking there must have been an R&B club close by from the way they were dressed, I figured my tattooed arms were a bit intimidating for them. As I went to take another spicy bite, I saw the blood on my hand from my cuts and then realised my face was also splattered with the stage blood. I laughed to myself, thinking I would have probably steered clear as well.

I quickly finished and walked back through Chinatown, witnessing three separate fistfights on the streets as I walked swiftly, glancing at the street map tucked in my hand. As I approached the hotel at 3am, my roommates Eric and Mel sent me a text saying they were heading back to the hotel from Iguana Bar too. It was perfect timing as I was hoping I wouldn't disturb them when I opened the door.

I took the opportunity to shower and I scrubbed the blood off me with soap and a hand towel. Thinking it was odd that I had not had an alcoholic beverage all night, I made myself a cup of tea and hopped into bed, looking through the sequence of photos on my camera from the adventures thus far and reflecting on what was my first-ever Mötley concert. It was a day I shall never forget!

MÖTLEY CRÜE
ALL ACCESS
MÖTLEY CRÜE
PAUL MILES
10TH STREET

Sunday, December 4, 2005 - Sydney to Brisbane

As I awoke, Tommy Lee's lyric of "This is Sunday, just another Sunday" filled my head, but I soon realised where I was and how different my world was this day. We packed up our belongings and checked out of the hotel, heading into Chinatown in search of a bacon and egg breakfast. We stopped at a café opposite Paddy's Markets on Ultimo Road and soaked up the late morning sunshine and breeze. Even with extra bacon, the serve was not as large or tasty as what I was used to in Melbourne.

A little further down the road, I bid farewell to Eric and Mel as they headed for the train station to get to the airport for their return flight home. My flight was not until a bit later in the afternoon so I had a couple of hours to kill in the city before I also needed to head to the airport. I strolled the streets, looking in shop windows as I ventured further downtown.

The shaded lawns of Hyde Park looked an ideal quiet spot to give my wife a call and bring her up to speed on my adventures, while seeing how she was coping with my son's sleepover party. Almost an hour later, I started to head towards Circular Quay on Sydney Harbour, intent on stealing some views of the Opera House and Harbour Bridge before boarding a train to the airport.

Since the InterContinental hotel was on my way down Macquarie Street, I thought I would walk by and see if any of the band or crew were perhaps around, since I was going that way anyway. On the corner outside the hotel, I noticed one of the Crüe's dancers walking towards me, having just come out of the hotel complex. It was Jozie Di Maria. We quickly sized each other up before striking a conversation.

I soon told her that I would probably see her around some more as I was doing all six shows of the band's Australian tour, continuing that I live in Melbourne after having moved there from Perth five years ago. Jozie grabbed my arm and looked into my eyes from behind her reflective aviator sunglasses. "Dude, you have to take me to Bon Scott's grave when we get to Perth." With surprise, I said I surely would as Nikki and I have already chatted about that and we planned on going. Jozie said that ever since she found out the tour would be going to Australia and included Perth; Bon's grave was top of her list of things to do.

As I made a promise to take her, she said she was going to the store and that I should walk with her. Inside the store she asked me about the goodness of various nutritional food bars as I sipped on a cold drink to quench my thirst from all the city walking. "Where's the yoghurt Paul?"

As Jozie paid for her items, grabbing more and more as they were being scanned, she asked where I was headed now. I told her that I was on the same 2:05pm flight to Brisbane as her and the band, so I needed to go catch a train to the airport next. She said I should walk back to the hotel with her, as they would have room for me to travel with them instead. Sounded good to me.

Happy to put my heavy bag down, Jozie introduced me to fellow dancer Brandy and I said hello to Alecia who was sitting in the vehicle, ready to roll. Nikki soon came out and we exchanged some small talk before he got into a Mercedes with Kimo. The rest of the band then came out and got into their respective sedans. As the vehicle that Jozie was to ride in started to fill with crew bodies, she was told there'd be no room for me to ride with them. Disappointed and uncomfortable, I started to walk away thinking that I'd better hurry to the train station.

A management-looking guy then said I could ride in that vehicle, pointing to another similar sized Tarago. I hastily walked over and opened the sliding door and got in, surprised to find only a driver and front-seat passenger occupying the otherwise empty people mover. I thanked them for giving me a ride and introduced myself. The other passenger was the promoter himself, Andrew McManus. A few questions about the tour's progress to date punctuated the otherwise general chitchat and silence of thought. Andrew told us that two local workers suffered heart attacks inside the arena last night.

Most vehicles arrived at Sydney airport's Group Check-in zone at pretty much the same time. Tour Manager Jack Carson must have arrived earlier as he was handing out boarding passes to crewmembers. Knowing that I had to check-in, as there wouldn't be a boarding pass for me in Jack's hands, I quickly approached the Qantas counter, keen to get it sorted before the others went a separate way. As I handed over my Frequent Flyer card, I asked the lady to please seat me with them. My boarding pass showed I was to sit in the fourth row, behind the first three of first class.

As I turned from the counter, I noticed Vince Neil had taken a seat inside the building as the last of hand luggage was removed from the vehicles. I took the opportunity to introduce myself and have a chat, but he seemed a bit distant and un-talkative, so I left him to be. He looked more sunburned than I thought he was. Ouch.

The traveling party then made its way through the airport terminal with photo and autograph seeking fans doing their best to get amongst the limited action. I went with the flow and soon entered the Qantas Club lounge with the others.

I reacquainted myself with Mick Mars, Rhyno and Tam, sitting with them as we snacked. It was great to enjoy first hand the many wisecracks and humourous dialogue from Mick's mouth as he slouched awkwardly but most comfortably in the tub chair.

Mick was saying he had some ideas of what Mighty Mike could do at forthcoming shows, at the part in the show where Mick is introduced on stage and the little guy comes out and does something crazy. Mick said he wanted a real Eucalyptus tree on stage, so Mighty Mike could dress up as a koala and fall out of the tree onto the stage. Someone said he could also dress in a kangaroo costume; Mick quickly pointed out it would be a wallaby costume as Mighty Mike is too small to be a kangaroo. I was impressed at Mick's knowledge of Australian fauna.

Nikki and others wandered from seat to seat to buffet, enjoying the carrot soup, and joining in general conversation. Tommy spent most of the time chatting with Andrew McManus before Nikki joined them. Vince and his bodyguard Ray were the only ones to sit well away from the main group. I wondered to myself if something was up, or if that was normal.

Time ticked away as our flight was delayed and various members of the touring party started to pass comment of their annoyance at the delay. It was certainly fine by me; I got to sit around with them longer and enjoy more and more of Mick's time-killing ramblings. I also spent a lot of time chatting with Mighty Mike (Mike Murga), learning about his Czech background and his current studies and other activities being pursued between work commitments.

Nikki sat in his tub chair with an incense stick burning away, held in his hand like a cigarette. A member of staff saw the smoke and courteously told him that it was a non-smoking area. Nikki told her that he wasn't smoking and when she looked back at him puzzled, he held his hand up higher and said that it was incense. She apologised profusely, knowing he was a celebrity, and then walked away, clearly with some embarrassment. Nikki then put the incense stick to his mouth and started to draw on it like a cigarette. Everyone was laughing.

I said a hello to Tommy as he passed by me on the way to the buffet for a last bite, before we soon headed out of the lounge and towards the boarding gate. Fans once again congregated and followed, seeking opportunities to get an item signed and snap a photo. Nikki signed a few; Rhyno said Mick doesn't sign in airports.

We boarded the plane and I made my way to my seat in the fourth row. Screens in front of me blocked any views of the four Mötley band members occupying their seats in the first class rows in front of me. You could feel a buzz on the plane as passengers passed on word to others that Mötley Crüe members were the celebrities they were flying with.

The couple seated next to me recognised Tommy Lee and were keen to talk about everything that was happening. Before we landed in Brisbane, I learnt he was a banker who owned many properties throughout Queensland and was returning from a holiday in Tasmania with his partner. I politely turned down an offer of as much marijuana that I felt like during my stay in Brisbane.

After landing in Brisbane and disembarking the plane, the rise in temperature and humidity was instantly noticeable as we walked the aero-bridge corridor towards the arrivals lounge. I was chatting with Nikki as we entered the public area and were faced with more fans eager to meet their heroes, with cameras and sharpie pens at the ready.

As I backed away, one fan approached and asked me for an autograph, passing me a pen and single sheet of folded paper. I laughed under my breath and obliged, signing my name and writing CrueTime.com underneath, thinking it may help ease any confusion when they try and work out who I actually was.

Shinbone also greeted me at the airport, along with my former business partner and friend Dean Boswell from Melbourne. Jozie checked with me that I was cool for a ride to the band's hotel before she left the terminal and I told her I'd see her at the Sofitel where I was also going to be staying, sharing the room of Shinbone and his girlfriend Vicky.

Driving into the city of Brisbane, we exchanged stories of our tour experiences to date as I looked out at some of the familiar sights that brought back memories of my four months living there during 1993. Familiar faces from the touring party were seen all around as we pulled off Turbot Street and into the hotel, passing the customary fans outside on the way in to check-in.

Entering the foyer, I saw my friend from the Gold Coast, Jason Mayne and his wife, who were also staying at the hotel and were keen to see Alecia again, having met in Las Vegas earlier in the year. I asked them to give me some time to get organised and I'd be back down to catch up with them some more.

The hotel room soon turned into a party as many mates of Shinbone came up for pre-show drinks. The afternoon ticked by quickly and I was conscious of wanting to get to the venue as early as possible, since I missed some action last night in Sydney while waiting for tickets and passes. Shinbone was driving to the venue so I was comfortable I'd have a seat in his car, but it seemed there were more people than cars.

Jason was encouraging me to share some shots of Jagermeister with him for old time's sake, but I stood my ground and refused, not forgetting the last time we did that in Melbourne together and we both ended up heaving. That's the last thing I wanted to be doing tonight.

We finally arrived at the venue located back near the airport and we made our way from the large carpark through the sticky tropical weather towards the entrance. I again had my camera in my pocket but could not be bothered trying to stow in my jocks, so I told Shinbone that I was going to enter through a separate stage door and meet back up with him in the bar.

Inside the venue's foyer, I noticed a lot more tattoos on the punters. Perhaps the warmer weather meant I was seeing more skin and therefore more opportunity to see tatts? Maybe it's a cultural difference of Brisbane? Interesting.

I met up with Shinbone and the rest of his mates in the bar, but I was feeling uncomfortable. I didn't really want to spend ages queuing in lines to get alcohol, especially with his mates that I didn't really know, or have time to get to know better. I wanted to head backstage but I knew that I'd need to escort Shinbone with me and any other friends of his that had VIP passes. I felt we got kicked out last night in Sydney before the show because there were too many people hanging around. So I thought I'd head back and get a feel for it; perhaps it would be different back there tonight, perhaps it may be appropriate for lots of people to come through now. Shinbone was also feeling the pressure of all his mates' attention.

Backstage, I said hello to some of the familiar faces from the night before. I felt more comfortable that they were seeing just me there this time. I walked the corridors to the very loud dance beats vibrating through the walls of Tommy Lee's dressing room, and scoped out where the best access points were to the stage and to the floor of the venue.

Kimo said Nikki was getting ready for the show so I said I'd grab a bite to eat and be back soon. I remembered Nikki mentioning last night that there was 'real food' in catering, so I found the room and headed to the buffet. I was soon sitting at a table eating Barramundi fish in a lovely sauce, slices of roast turkey breast with gravy and more. I grabbed a can of Coke from the shop-style fridge and thought that this was much better than standing in line for some XXXX beer with guys I didn't know wanting to tell me their tales.

Full and much more comfortable, except for the sticky climate, I headed back down the corridors again and heard the muffled sounds of Motörhead at about 8:15pm. Having missed them the previous night, I entered the arena floor and managed to catch most of Ace Of Spades and then Overkill. Wow! Impressive.

As the house lights came back on after their set, I headed backstage again, bumping into the guys from The Casanovas. I walked back up the corridor and had a yak with Kimo before Nikki opened his dressing room door and joined us, now ready for the show. "Ten minutes" came the call from down the corridor to the band member's minders. Sixx swaggered as he talked. You could see the anticipation in his eyes beaming through his red bandit makeup. It was the first I'd seen Sixx with his face-full of stage makeup. Cool… the evil fucker.

"Five minutes!" He was moving like a caged animal about to be let loose. After confessing to me that he's not fond of showers, I snickered to myself as I wondered if the talcum powder all over him was for a cool stage appearance or really to make him smell nice. With just three minutes to go, I reached into my pocket and pulled out my camera. I swiveled the screen and held it out in front of us, making sure our heads were in frame. Flash! Nice.

The other band members soon came out of their dressing rooms too and the performers all moved down the corridor together towards the stage entry. I hung back to not get in anyone's way and followed them all the way, thinking that this is something I missed last night.

With their two-hour show about to commence at 9pm, I headed out onto the general admission floor area of the Brisbane Entertainment Centre. The crowd was packed in tight and since I was already feeling sweaty, I thought I would watch the show from the wings more tonight and not get in the pit.

The show was the same, yet it certainly felt different the second time around. Feeling free, I wandered to different parts of the area, witnessing different songs from different angles. I sat in the 'Stevie Wonder seats' for On With The Show. I stood at the sound desk at the back of the floor and enjoyed the awesome strobe lights during Live Wire. I was side of stage when Girls, Girls, Girls started and got a full view of the motorbike crash as it was making its way out on stage. I took some time to watch the video screens and the footage they showed, especially enjoying the wedding movie during Same Ol' Situation that features the dancers and Mighty Mike.

Whilst the Brisbane crowd was clearly smaller than the previous night in Sydney, they seemed probably just as loud. Of the opinion that Sydney was subdued, I was now thinking that this was more how I had expected audiences to react. Sixx approached the microphone and yelled, "I have three words for you… Aussie! Aussie! Aussie!" The crowd responded with a very loud, "Oi! Oi! Oi!" Excellent – we knew it would work well.

As the concert came to a close, I once again headed backstage to the dressing rooms. Conscious that Shinbone and the others would want to come backstage too, I thought I'd try and quickly sum up the situation and the possibilities.

In the corridor, I was about to pass the familiar face of a sharp-dressed man standing with a beautiful Asian lady holding a very cute little child with big, white ear muffs on. We kind of looked at each other and stopped to say hello. They recognised me from Melbourne airport the other day and I asked if he was Perry. Indeed it was Perry Farrell from Jane's Addiction and

Porno For Pyro's; I wasn't imagining things the other day. He said he was in Australia to DJ at some Earthcore festivals. We chatted for a little while before I continued down the corridor to see where the Mötley guys were.

Vince had told Nikki on stage that he was splitting right after the show and going back down to the Gold Coast. It seems Mick always exits the venue as soon as possible after the show and Nikki was also keen to leave ASAP.

That left Tommy, who had his dance music pumping through the walls and corridors once more. Everyone was soon called into Tommy's room to have cake for his personal assistant's birthday. I didn't feel I should join them, so I took it as a cue to leave and find Shinbone, Vicky and the others.

I informed them of the situation when I caught up with them and conveyed that I didn't think there would be a chance to hang with Nikki tonight. Shinbone was a bit annoyed that I had not taken him backstage pre-show as he said he was hungry and could have done with a catering visit. He wanted me to take him back to get some food now but I told him that I saw the catering buffets had closed long ago and there was no food around.

The only action backstage was Tommy Lee's assistant Tony Sullivan guiding through many young girls with passes to join the queue outside the drummer's dressing room door. Without tits, this only backstage activity was of no access to Shinbone and his male companions.

As the group of people sat on and around a couch for quite some time, Shinbone was displeased with the situation and I was displeased with the sticky Brisbane heat. They finally agreed it was time to walk to the car and head back to the city hotel, talking about the concert on the half-hour drive.

Mighty Mike was keen to kick on with us tonight and I left it to Shinbone in his hometown to guide us to the best action spots. There had been talk of a Tommy Lee DJ performance at Chalk; the Regatta Club was mentioned. A friend of Shinbone phoned him as we met Mighty Mike in the lobby. They were at a nearby strip club, shooting some pool with Mr. Lemmy Kilmister from Motörhead.

Confident that they thought this was our best option for a drink on a Sunday night after 1am, we headed down the warm city streets on a promise that it was 'just around the corner.' The walk seemed to continue forever and Mighty Mike was sweating and tired, having only had one hour's sleep the previous night. We checked out a giant Christmas tree that we passed on the way, Dean and I stopping for a photo with Mighty Mike in front of it.

After finally arriving at the strip club, the girl at the counter said it was $15 for entry. There were six or seven of us who said that was just not going to happen. We settled on a deal of $5 each and Shinbone handed over the money, telling us we all had to buy him a drink once inside. Entering the dark, thinly populated club, I spotted Lemmy at the bar talking to some scantily clad ladies.

I was talking to Shinbone's girlfriend Vicky as we waited on our first drinks to be served, when I noticed Lemmy and the girls walking towards the back of the venue before disappearing out of view. Shinbone soon told us that the door-girl came up to him and refunded the entry money, saying she was sorry that she didn't realise we were VIPs and drinks were on the house for us tonight.

Mighty Mike and I sat on stools at a vacant round table towards the front of the dragstrip, sipping our drinks for some cool relief. Thankfully, the poor quality and quantity of the girls that performed prevented us from getting any hotter. Lemmy returned to the bar after more than an hour.

Soon, Dean was encouraging me to come and have a chat with the man, but by this time I was not really in the mood for talking much. One of Shinbone's friends was particularly obnoxious and annoying the hell out of me by picking up my drink from in between my arms on the table right in front of me, insisting it was his. I was ready to clock him if he did it a third time. Mighty Mike was falling asleep in his drink, so we decided it was a good time to head back to the Sofitel for some sleep. We'd had more than enough to drink.

The walk back to the hotel seemed even longer than the journey there. Mighty Mike was cursing, telling us he was walking double what we are. I offered the four-foot-three guy a piggyback but I got the impression little people do not like such concessions.

We said goodbye to Mike in the hotel elevator and headed back to our hotel room. Shinbone and Vicky shared a bed, while I had the other. Dean was left with a key to crash on the floor once he'd had enough drinking with friend JJ Speedball and Motörhead's Lemmy. I thought, knowing Dean, we may not see him until check out.

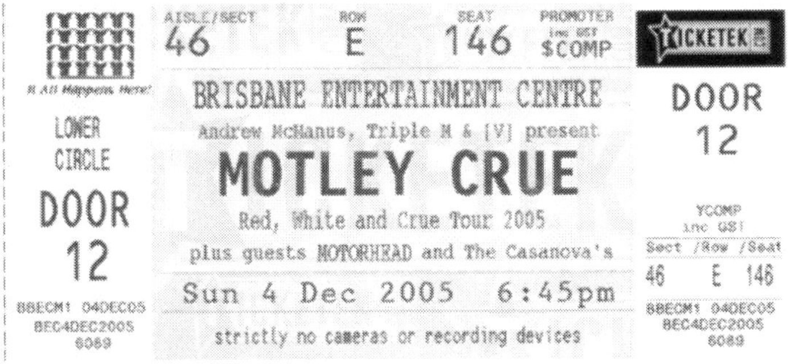
AISLE/SECT
46
ROW
E
SEAT
146
PROMOTER
$COMP
TICKETEK
LOWER
CIRCLE
DOOR
12
BRISBANE ENTERTAINMENT CENTRE
Andrew McManus, Triple M & [V] present
MOTLEY CRUE
Red, White and Crue Tour 2005
plus guests MOTORHEAD and The Casanova's
Sun 4 Dec 2005 6:45pm
strictly no cameras or recording devices
DOOR
12
Sect /Row /Seat
46 E 146
88ECM1 04DEC05
8EC4DEC2005
6069

CARNIVAL OF SINS
MÖTLEY CRÜE
VIP
4 DEC 05 BRS

MÖTLEY CRÜE

Sunday, Dec 4, 2005

ENTERTAINMENT CENTER
BRISBANE, AUSTRALIA

Sound Check: TBA

DINNER: 5:00 pm

DOORS: 6:30 pm

THE CASSANOVA'S 7:00 – 7:20

MOTORHEAD 7:40 – 8:30

MÖTLEY CRÜE 9:00

Curfew – 11:00 PM

AFTERSHOW TRAVEL

TRAVEL TO BRISBANE HOTEL
FLY TO MELBOURNE IN THE MORNING

Monday, December 5, 2005 - Brisbane to Melbourne

Disturbed by noises in the room, I forced one eye open. As the fuzzy view came into picture, I saw Shinbone and Vicky about ready to leave the hotel room. It was perhaps around 8am and they were on their way to catch an early flight to Melbourne. They said goodbye and reminded me to hand in the other key on my check out. I told them I'd see them down in Melbourne later on.

I could hear snoring. A turn of my heavy head gave me view of a fully clothed Dean, flat on his back on Shinbone's bed, mouth wide open. I set the alarm on my mobile phone and went back to sleep. I felt much better for the additional hours of sleep I got before waking again. I stirred Dean a few times as I showered, dressed and packed my bag.

We left the room and headed down to the lobby, with Dean telling me about his adventures with Lemmy at the Casino after the strip club and how JJ was stripping on the stage before they left. However, I was comfortable that I left at the right time, as he didn't get back until 7am or so.

I told Dean I would see if I could ride with the band's vehicles to the airport, as he left to make his own way there. With time to kill until my 1:50pm flight, I caught up with Jason and Natalie again in the lobby.

Shortly before 11am, Lemmy strolled out of the lifts and across the lobby towards the bar, sipping from his glass of whisky as a couple of fans approached him for a signature and photo. I had been told that he drinks two bottles of Jack Daniel's a day and his doctor said that he will die if he stops now. I was watching his routine of staying alive and kicking.

Sitting in the lobby, I had the opportunity to have a good conversation with Pedro Pineda, the guy hired to film as much documentary footage of the band and the tour as possible. We'd exchanged pleasantries previously on the tour before but we got to know one another a lot more. As we talked, he prepared his cameras for the new day ahead, wiping them all over as he tried to remove the birthday cake enjoyed backstage the previous night. He captured the massive food fight on camera and had the chocolate remnants to prove it.

We were amazed to find out we both have a background in solid plastering, as we sat discussing hawks, trowels, mixing render in wheelbarrows and sand finish. He said he first met Nikki when contracted to perform some maintenance on his house back in the mid-eighties and he then worked on Vince's house, then Tommy and Heather's house up on the hill.

I was asking some questions about his cameras and equipment when he said that perhaps I could shoot some footage at one of the shows, as it's always good to get a different perspective. I said that the Adelaide show would probably be best and we agreed to see how that pans out when we get there.

Nikki soon came down for lobby call and said hello, chatting for a while and signing items and having photos with some fans, before he headed off to the airport. Jozie said I should be fine to ride in the vehicle to the airport. Thankfully it was a six-seater this time. Pedro sat in the front, while Alecia tried to get comfortable on the back seat without aggravating her new flower tattoo on her hip, with Mighty Mike and Brandy next to her. I sat on the middle bench seat with Jozie and Chris, who seemed like he was in charge of seating logistics and was not really talkative, probably wondering who the hell I was. He was called 'C-Money' by the crew – Chris Risner, the Tour Accountant.

On the way to the airport, we looked at digital camera photos of the cake fight and laughed at the stories. I liked the snaps of Tommy and Nikki's faces covered in it. Mighty Mike and I shared some tales of our strip club adventures the previous night.

Arriving at the airport, I quickly made my way to check-in as the band was going through the security scanners. I was pleased to see I was again seated in the fourth row. With boarding pass now in hand and not wanting to lose touch with the main group, I quickly emptied the contents of my pockets into a tray, putting it on the x-ray conveyor with my hand-luggage bag.

I beeped as I walked through, so the lady instructed me to take my cotton cap off; whatever. I beeped again. This time she told me I needed to take my shoes off. Damn. I beeped again, and again, and again. Feeling rather naked, I finally made it silently through the scanners and got dressed again as fast as I could.

A couple of fans stopped me at the top of the elevator and asked for an autograph. Weird. Did they know who I am and wanted me to sign their paper, or did they perhaps think I was one of the band members? Or did I look like a rock'n'roll type that could have been someone famous so they took a chance? It confused me but I didn't really want to engage in conversation to ask as I was thinking about where the others had gone. I signed for them and headed towards the Qantas Club lounge hoping they wouldn't want to check for my access since I wasn't walking in with the main group.

I managed to catch up to Mighty Mike, and then Jack, Nikki and Kimo. With Nikki stopping into a newsagency to browse some shelves, Jack, Kimo and I waited outside. Kimo scolded a fan for taking photos of Nikki shopping, as I asked Jack if I could go into the lounge. He said he had organised access for the touring party and if I was a Qantas Club member I could go through. I wasn't, damn.

I noticed Patrick Prendergast from Andrew McManus Presents was standing at the lounge entry desk, so I wandered away from Jack and Kimo as Nikki still shopped. As I approached, Patrick told the staff that I was to go through - excellent. Spotting the main group, I placed my hand luggage at the side of an empty chair next to Mick Mars, relieved that I could now chill out and hopefully enjoy some more airport lounge gags from Mick. It started immediately.

Telling Mick of my hassles in coming through the security, he quickly became animated as he re-enacted his own conversation with the security lady who wanted him to keep removing items until he beeped no more. "I told her at least five fucking times that I've had a fucking hip replacement and of course I'm going to fucking beep… that fucking bitch. I can't take my fucking leg off and put it on the fucking conveyor... that fucking bitch." I was glad that Mick's nurse Tam was sitting with us, just incase he burst a blood vessel. Ah, Mick. I was enjoying my day.

Soup seemed to be the biggest hit on offer with the party again, but I was after something cold, pleased that I would now be escaping the humid Brisbane conditions.

Sitting there casually chatting with different members of the touring party, I couldn't help but notice the reactions of other members of the lounge waiting for their flights. Whether they recognised any of the other band members, most certainly knew celebrities were present due to the burly presence of the security lads, not to mention Pedro's professional-looking camera capturing the events.

I observed their glances, whispers to the person next to them, then longer stares from more people. Some would take the long way to the buffet, just to walk slowly past, hoping to catch some celebrity conversation. Some brave enough would approach for an autograph, as others asked non-famous looking members of the traveling party who they were traveling with. It was all very interesting to watch, and to be a part of. I enjoyed it, and was eager to experience more of it.

At one point, I looked across and noticed Mick looking at me. He held up two fingers at me like a peace sign before bending them forward a little. With a wry smile on his face, he said to me, "You know what this is?" I copied his hand sign and then turned it around like I was going to poke myself in the eyes. He said, "You got it. It's an eye gouger!" We laughed and it was cool that our minds thought alike and I understood his charade first go. As the tour progressed, it became our little hand sign that we'd flash at each other.

The flight was again delayed but I didn't care of course. I heard the delay was due to them needing to fix a hole in the runway. I figured it was a joke to help alleviate the crew's frustration of sitting around the airport.

Tommy Lee was not with us as he was to DJ at a venue called Home in Sydney tonight. With Vince Neil currently enjoying his day off on the Gold Coast, Mick, Nikki and the crew spent their day off traveling and started to pick on tour manager Jack Carson, asking him to get them a beach so they could be like Vince. Nikki was in the thick of it. "Hey Jack, do they hire jet skis at this beach?" Kimo asked Nikki if he wanted his beach umbrella moved a little. The ragging and jokes continued until it was time to leave the beach and head for the boarding gate.

I walked with Nikki and Kimo as fans tried to capitalise on autograph and photo opportunities on the way. Nikki had mentioned before the tour that he was keen to eat some crocodile again with me this tour, and I told him that tonight in Melbourne might be the best opportunity for that. However since we were due to touch down at 5:10pm and we were now delayed even more, we weren't sure how the night would play out for a meal. Since I would be going home once we arrived in Melbourne, he suggested I give him a call later, once he's settled in his hotel room at Crown Towers and we can see what's best from there.

Sitting on the plane, my view of the first class rows in front of me were unfortunately obscured by screens again. I thought about some of the Mötley items in my hand luggage that I packed in hope to get signed, and then reflected on how the guys are constantly approached whenever they are in public space outside the no-go zones of restricted access. I reflected on how I felt that I had now entered the inside of the tour, having passed through real and virtual barriers that keep fans from entering their private space. For me to ask for any autographs from them just didn't feel right; in fact, it felt wrong.

The items remained protected in my bag as I ate my aeroplane food with headphones on to prevent engaging in conversation from those curious folk occupying seats around me. As the jet's music program on Channel 6 played Dr.

Feelgood followed by Ace Of Spades, I said a big 'Fuck yeah' to myself, knowing I was flying high with the Crüe. I felt proud of what I had achieved, excited that my hard work over many years was now paying some dividends, and I was only two shows into the tour.

Disembarking the plane in Melbourne, I walked past Mick slumped in seat 1A as he waited for Rhyno and Tam; I gave him the gouging fingers sign. He laughed and we exchanged smiles as I said "Seeya Captain," laughing to myself having recalled a situation from before we left. Mick had showed me his seat 1A boarding pass in the lounge and when I commented, "You can't get a better seat than that mate" he retorted, "Oh yes you can. I could be flying the fucking jet!"

I caught up with Nikki and Kimo just ahead and we soon entered public space again, greeted by the usual flashing of fan cameras and waving of black sharpies. Nikki found a balance of giving fans what they wanted but going about his business in a sensible way.

As we walked and then stood on the travelator, Nikki was gently kicking my bag from behind, saying, "Hey stalker, get out the way." I turned around and smiled at him as he continued Tommy's joke from the press conference. He had called me 'stalker' a few times now, always with a cheeky grin on his face. We continued hastily towards the designated area of the vehicles and when he said that I should ride with him this time I said, "Sure."

I sat in the back seat of the black sedan with Nikki; Kimo in the front. More cameras flashed through the dark-tinted window as we pulled out from the kerb. We laughed at the lengths fans go to in catching a glimpse of band members as a couple of guys in Mötley shirts ran up the pathway alongside the vehicle for some length. I silently thought about what lengths I had gone to in earning my thirty minutes of private one-on-one conversation with the band's leader as we made our way into my city.

We talked about many things on that backseat. Probably half of it was Mötley-related; the other half was just general talk about… life. We talked a lot about our families. Nikki's eldest son Gunner is just a couple of months apart in age with my son Ben, so we talked about their characteristics and behaviour at this age and our parenting tactics to positively discipline and encourage them to do their best. With my twenty-year-old daughter now moved out of home and Nikki's eldest daughter knocking on puberty's door, we laughed at different strategies used and yet to be implemented of keeping the boys at bay from our girls. Nikki said he was looking forward to catching up with my wife Sara again.

I told Nikki it was great to be able to have the time to spend with him. Through my work on the band over the last ten years, I felt that I knew Nikki reasonably well but this was a good chance for him to learn some more about me. He agreed wholeheartedly, but also said that I probably don't really know him as a person that well yet. He was right, even though we had previously met once before during our ten years of communicating with each other. From watching countless interviews with him and reading even more interviews, I felt I knew the public Nikki very well, but not the private Nikki. That difference is important and I was pleased I was getting to know the real Nikki Sixx.

As we enjoyed the freeway approach into Melbourne, my mind also wandered with thoughts about the conversations we were having, feeling this whole experience was not a business-thing, not a fan-thing, but more of a conversation that friends would typically share. I was aware that so often your idols can let you down massively upon meeting them, as illustrated by Nikki's own bad experiences with Brian Connolly of the Sweet. As I sat with MY hero, I was thankful that mine was also a genuine, caring, down-to-earth, regular guy that actually felt like more of a friend than other people that I know in my city and would call a friend.

Arriving at Crown, we were met by the routine of camera flashing and sharpie-holding fans, requesting snaps and squiggles on Mötley merchandise. Nikki moved quickly and I left him with a promise that I'd call later as he headed off to the solace of his hotel room.

Shinbone and Vicky were in the foyer and they called out to me from the couch they were sitting on, dressed for a night out. During a brief chat, I brought them up to speed on dinner plans, keen to head home to see my family for a while as the hectic pace continued.

In the short taxi ride to my 17th floor apartment, I took some time to respond to some of the flood of SMS messages on my mobile phone from the last few days, hoping to appease and not wanting to disappoint any acquaintances that were counting on me to provide them with opportunity to get closer to the band in some way.

It was great to see my wife and son again. Whilst we enjoy a rare adventure on our own, we always find it horrible to be away from each other. I caught them up on some more of what I had been up to, as I unpacked my dirty laundry and looked forward to my own pillow that night.

As time ticked by, we started getting ready for dinner, regardless of whether Nikki would be joining us or not. I soon gave him a call, only to leave a voicemail for him to return. We taxied our way into the hotel and I gave him another call from the foyer, having the best Indigenous restaurant in Melbourne (and probably Australia) on a standby booking just a short drive away in Carlton.

Nikki didn't feel like going out of the hotel complex, suggesting we maybe go to the Japanese restaurant on level three of the Crown complex; fine by us. Sara and I had been to Koko's before and knew that it was certainly one of the city's best Japanese restaurants and Japanese was certainly one of our favourite foods (check it out at www.kokoatcrown.com.au). I checked with Shinbone and Vicky who had met us in the lobby and they of course said it sounded fine to them. Pedro was also ready for a night out with us, minus his camera for once.

We met Nikki and Kimo on level three in ten minutes, once our friends Ron and Leah had joined us. They dined with Nikki and us last year and were keen to catch up with Nikki again, especially considering his recent trip to Cambodia. Leah was planning to head there to lend a caring hand a few years ago, until she met Ron, fell in love and married him. Since then she has gained a lot of experience coordinating and managing events and production projects and is now ready to use those skills towards helping out in Cambodia.

Our party of nine was shown to a beautiful private Teppanyaki dining area where we explored the delicious menu. After much decision, we chose to get a variety of dishes to share, expertly cooked in front of us by our chef for the evening. Chicken, prawns (including the crispy head and legs for those game enough like me), beef, garlic rice; it was all there, except the abalone that they forgot.

As we watched the chef cook our dinner, Nikki was saying it would be great to have one of these big hot plates at home. I was telling him how Sara is a great cook and he said Donna was too. We talked about our favourite meals and the best roast vegetables and he was telling us that whenever he tries to cook for the family he just can't seem to get the timing of everything right so the full meal is on the plate when served. With appetites satisfied and the restaurant winding down, we put our shoes back on and thanked Nikki.

As Nikki and I led the way out of the restaurant, I told him of an idea that I'd had spinning in my mind for some time, and for some reason it surfaced again at that point. I told him that Mötley and another band should perhaps record the same song but with separate vocals tracks so that when the songs are synched together, it sounds like a duet of sorts. Mötley would release it as a single, as would the other band, and with all the audio software available today fans could have fun merging the two songs together to hear what it sounds like as the one piece. Radio would probably have fun with it. Perhaps a cover of Love Me Two Times by The Doors would work. I told Nikki that I thought Aerosmith would be a great band to do such a project with. He looked at me and tilted his head slightly to the side and said, "And why Aerosmith?" "Because they're legends and I reckon it would be extremely cool," I replied. "Interesting," he said with a smile, "very, very interesting."

The others soon joined us outside the restaurant. Nikki and Kimo said they look forward to seeing us at the show tomorrow before they headed back to their rooms in the hotel, while we ventured to a bar across the road at Crown Promenade where the crew was staying. I introduced Mighty Mike to Sara and we drank with him there until the bar closed. We headed back across to the casino for some more drinks to close out the night, saying goodbye to last few remaining when we caught a taxi home.

Even though there was no Mötley Crüe concert tonight, it had still been a full day brimming with great, memorable times. It was good to finally crash in our bed with my own pillow. Thank goodness there was to be no alarm in the morning; I needed some decent sleep.

Tuesday, December 6, 2005 - Melbourne

After a good solid sleep, Sara and I spent the day at home, catching up on more normal tasks and responsibilities that were lagging with our different routines of the past few days. Before we knew it, it was approaching late afternoon and time to start getting ready for the show, in between phone calls from friends wanting to catch up for drinks.

My buddy Jason also called and told me that he finally managed to have a good catch up with Vince at the Sheraton on the Gold Coast last night, finding him poolside, then arranging to meet him in the lobby bar at 5pm before they drank wine together until 11pm or so, including some bottles of Vince's Vineyards that Jason brought along. Vince signed a bottle for him.

We left for Vodafone Arena, again later than I wanted to. With Foo Fighters playing at Rod Laver Arena next door, the traffic was chaotic. The persistent rain did not help the cause and our normal $8 taxi ride turned into about $20. As we inched closer to the show my frustration increased, while Sara told me to chill. I hate traffic… and I hate missed opportunities.

Upon arrival at the arena, we headed to the ticket window to pick up tickets and an All Access pass for Sara. Again, they weren't ready for us and it was already 7pm, the time that Nikki said we should meet him in his dressing room. We made our way into the venue and chatted with friends in the lobby for a moment, but we needed to sort out the pass for Sara. Jason also looked in danger of missing his Meet and Greet once more, since his items were also not at the ticket window as expected.

We asked many of the venue's staff if they could point us to the best way to the backstage area but incredibly none of them knew. I poked my head into the First Aid room hoping someone in there would know. We were in luck as a woman showed us the way to the correct elevator. Walking through the rabbit warren of corridors, we finally found the band's management staff and asked about the passes.

Todd asked us to wait while he tried to sort it out. We looked into the room that we were waiting outside of and saw the tail end of the Meet and Greet for Fanfire platinum package holders taking place. I saw quite a few familiar faces as they then filed out past us, including Sally and Pete. The band and their minders then came out and Nikki said to us, "Hey, I'll be back soon, don't go."

Todd took us into their management office and gave Sara a Support band pass, as he was unable to make up an All Access one as their laminator had broken earlier on this leg of the tour. After thanking Todd for his assistance, we then made our way to Nikki's dressing room. We chatted for a short while before I thought of Shinbone and Vicky again. I asked Nikki if I should go and get them and he said, "Sure." I said to Sara and Nikki that it was probably easiest if I just ducked out to find them and escort them back through. Nikki was fine with that so I made my way back out of the rabbit warren.

I was standing in the elevator heading up to the lobby level when it hit me. Oh no, what have I done? You see, when I met Sara in 1989 and we then married, she used to joke with me that since she couldn't marry Nikki Sixx, she had to marry me instead. It had been a bit of a running joke over the years. And now what had I done? I had left my wife backstage, alone with Nikki in his dressing room! Just as well we are faithful and trust each other one hundred percent.

I escorted Shinbone through with Vicky, who finally got to go backstage. We sat around Nikki's dressing room and chatted as he showed us his new cameras. As we chatted, Chris came in and said that Brandy was not feeling very well, but with some encouragement from Nikki she managed to soldier on and perform well in front of the sold-out crowd. Nikki told us that Vince was still on his way from the Gold Coast, cutting it fine time-wise by hiring a smaller private plane instead of taking his Qantas flight that was pre-arranged.

When we left Nikki's dressing room as it came time for him to prepare for the stage, he followed us out, probably to see if Vince had arrived, before taking some photos of us in the backstage corridors on his crazy new toy cameras. We then said goodbye and got a plate of beef pasta each in catering.

With twenty minutes until Mötley's show time, we heard some raised voices coming from the corridor as we sat down to eat. We then saw Vince walk into his dressing room and slam the door behind him. With five minutes to go, the door opened and Vince stepped into the corridor in his stage clothes and shouted down the corridor to someone at the other end, "See, I'm fucking ready. I'm fucking ready." With food in our bellies, Shinbone and Vicky went to their seats as Sara and I then watched the band members head out the corridor to the rear of the stage for their entry.

We then headed around the back of the stage and took our place amongst some road-cases and crewmembers watching from the side of the stage on Nikki's side. It was now finally Sara's time to enjoy her first Crüe show up close, but in a safe zone to avoid the sweat, bumps, knocks and general crush of the pit in front of the band.

Melbourne was easily the loudest of the concerts to date and you could see that the band, and Vince especially, was taken back with their enthusiasm. The crowd didn't need much encouragement to sing along, to punch the air with fists and to 'light the place up' with their cigarette lighters held high.

As Pantera's Cowboys From Hell played over the house speakers during the intermission, Sara and I headed backstage and caught Mighty Mike coming out of Tommy's dressing room with a Corona from his drinks rider. He ducked back inside and grabbed us one too and we had a chat for a little while. Venturing a little further down the corridor, we said hi to the guys from The Casanovas and their ladies before heading back out to the floor for the second half of the concert. After the motorbike spillage entering the stage in Brisbane, they did away with the bikes for the start of Girls, Girls, Girls.

Towards the end of the show, I needed to urinate. A song ended and I told Sara I was going to head to the toilets. At that point, the opening guitar sounds of Kickstart My Heart filled the arena. I stopped and decided to first watch this song instead. We watched Nikki smash his bass at the end of the song.

Through the darkness, I then saw Kimo walking towards me; a smashed up bass guitar being held in front of him by both his arms. He placed it on the road-case in front of me that I was leaning against and said, "Nikki said to make sure you get this." It took me completely by surprise – I had been knocked for six once again. I shook his hand, he gave me a hug and I thanked him, glad that I watched the song he played with it before smashing it, instead of relieving myself. In a state of shock, I ducked to the men's room and was back in time for the encore of Anarchy In The U.K.

It's strange how things work out some times, and it was certainly all rolling nicely for me. I recognised the thought that Nikki had given; not only did he know that I would absolutely love and appreciate the gesture and treasure the gift, he chose my hometown as the concert to do it, where I could also take the bass home instead of having to take it on board as hand-luggage if it was at another concert. How considerate.

As this was running through my mind while I stood there in amazement, the house lights came up and I heard people in the crowd calling out to me, thinking I was part of the crew and asking me to pass the broken bass up to them in the lower section of the stands behind us. As I was oblivious to it, Sara was turned around telling them, "No, it's his to keep. He's not handing anything over!"

When I turned around, I spotted my friend Rick Davies at the barricade on the side, so I moved over to greet him. He was blown away by the spectacle he had just witnessed. I told him that Sara and I were now heading backstage to see Nikki and I'd suss out if it was OK for him to pop back for a couple of minutes to meet Nikki and show him all his Crüe tattoos, including the Old English lettering of MOTLEY across his stomach, in the same style as Tommy Lee's MAYHEM tattoo.

We made our way back into Nikki's dressing room and I hugged him, thanking him for the bass. He was pleased that it gave me such a kick. After some more conversation, I asked if he minded if I brought my buddy Rick back for a moment to say a quick hello. Sixx obliged and I left Sara with Nikki again as I made my way back to the front of house barricade.

As I approached with a smile on my face and caught Rick's eyes, his face portrayed shock, disbelief, nervousness, and immense anticipation, all in the one priceless expression. I told security that I was escorting him backstage and as we walked through the corridors and doorways to Nikki's dressing room, I briefed him on what to expect and encouraged him to keep cool and calm. I knew what he was like; I remembered pulling him out of the pit in front of Nikki at the Brides of Destruction concert a year ago as he nearly fainted with the combination of awe, heat, dehydration, fluster and the moment. Rick kept his cool and greeted Nikki with a hug, stoked to finally meet his idol. Words were exchanged, tattoos were displayed, photos were taken of each other, and everything was perfect.

As time came for us to move on, I asked Nikki if he knew about, or was going to the 'official after-party' at Spearmint Rhyno strip club where it was promoted that the band would be present in a VIP area. Confirming my suspicions, Nikki said, "It ain't fucking official with me." We decided we'd head to Cherry bar to quench our thirst.

We said goodbyes and looked forward to enjoying another show together tomorrow. Walking along the corridor, we pulled over to one side as a seemingly heavily intoxicated Vince Neil passed us. Rick said a quick hello to him as he passed and Vince was obliging and said it was nice to meet him. As I stood next to Vince with Nikki's bass in my arms, Vince also said it was nice to meet me as well. Perhaps he didn't recognise me through the beer goggles he was wearing.

As we walked further down the corridor, a guy from Motörhead's Australian distributor Riot called me into the

Motörhead office. I had met him on the Brides of Destruction tour and we watched the show from the same area tonight, exchanging a few words after Don't Go Away Mad and both acknowledging it is one of the Crüe's finest tracks. He handed me a copy of the new Motörhead DVD. I thanked the big fella very much and was pleased that I had another souvenir to enjoy from the tour.

Exiting the elevator into a lobby alcove, we saw heavy rain through an outside window and all the people milling outside and taking shelter from it. We were planning on catching a taxi into the city but now that I had the broken bass in my arms we needed to head home, but there was no way I was going to go out near the public for fear of getting mobbed and the bass stolen. Even standing in a secluded part of the foyer, the odd fan that did straggle past was quick to spot it and ask for a string off it, anything I was willing to give. Sorry.

We called our friends Eric and Mel, who were about to leave in Geoff Robertson's car. They had room for us to squeeze in, so a drenched Eric soon returned from the carpark with a blanket from their boot for me to wrap the bass in. With a firm grip on the parcel covered in the thin black rubber underlay of the picnic blanket, we hastily left the foyer and headed to the carpark, not slowing or making eye contact with anyone. Putting the bass in the boot, I was thinking that people were probably thinking I had a dead body in the wrapping or something (even without a blood splattered face this night).

Soaked, we crammed into the car and all started laughing. Geoff drove us to our apartment and we said everyone should come up so they could have a look at it if they liked. Unwrapping it on the kitchen table, everyone stood around and admired the wreck of Sixx's handy-work, with the word FUCKER scratched into the black body of the Fender Squier P-bass. As a die-hard Crüehead, Geoff was keen to get a photo taken with it. After many thanks for the ride home to safety, they left and we dried off.

As I was still yet to catch up with my friend Adam from Newcastle, who I was on the way to visit in the tenth row the night of the Sydney show but never made it, I decided to give him a call and we arranged to meet. We picked him up in a taxi and headed to Cherry bar with Jason and his friend Colin. As usual, the bar was cranking with a cool rock vibe. I knew it would be; it's my favourite bar in Melbourne. As we stood around and drank in the back jungle room, Mikkey Dee and Phil Campbell from Motörhead and some of their crew also enjoyed the night.

Adam was a bit disappointed that he had not been able to see any of the Mötley guys before heading back to Sydney in the morning. He was also disappointed that his drum hero Tommy Lee did not perform a drum solo on the tour. He went up to Mikkey Dee and told him that Tommy had disappointed him by not doing a solo but Mikkey's solo kicked his ass; he made a new friend.

We chatted with Bobby Oberdorstein for a while, telling us stories of how he first came on board as Mick Mars' guitar tech towards the end of the Girls, Girls, Girls days. Adam thought it was great that a man that had a big influence on the guitar sounds of the Dr. Feelgood album was now drinking with us.

As 3 or 4am came around, the bar was closing for the night so it was time to head off. Bobby O jumped in our cab and we dropped him off at his hotel around the corner, followed by Adam at his hotel. Last stop was home and bed.

CARNIVAL OF SINS
MÖTLEY CRÜE
SUPPORT

VODAFONE ARENA
AT MELBOURNE PARK
Andrew McManus, Triple M
& Channel V present
MOTLEY CRUE
RED, WHITE & CRUE TOUR 2005
Plus guests Motorhead
NO PHOTOGRAPHY OR RECORDING DEVICES ALLOWED
Tue 6 Dec 2005 6:45pm
ENTER DOOR SECTION ROW SEAT COMP
4 18 LOWER F 81 $0.00
TICKETEK
ENTER DOOR 4
vodafone arena
SECTION 18 LOWER
VODAFONE ARENA
AT MELBOURNE PARK
Andrew McManus, Triple M
& Channel V present
MOTLEY CRUE
RED, WHITE & CRUE TOUR 2005
Plus guests Motorhead
Tue 6 Dec 2005 6:45pm
ENTER DOOR 2
SECTION GENERAL ADMISSION
COMP $0.00
vodafone arena
TICKETEK
ENTER DOOR 2

PAUL—
You're GREAT!
FUCKER

Wednesday, December 7, 2005 - Melbourne

Switching my phone off, we managed to get a good sleep until about lunchtime. Sara and I again took it easy during the afternoon before getting ready for the next show, this time at the intimate Palais Theatre in St Kilda.

Jason and Colin came over late in the afternoon and we sat around having some drinks, enjoying the balcony view. Shinbone and Vicky were to be joining us as well, but they were running late. Stressed at their day's events, they finally arrived, but it was already past the time that we wanted to leave to head to the show. One quick drink and we headed down to the tram stop out thc front.

As we arrived at the Palais Theatre, we were impressed by the 'Tonight – Mötley Crüe' marquee signage on the façade of the beautiful building built in 1927. I took some photos of the marquee while daylight was still with us. Mighty Mike rode up the side street to the front of the venue on his mini unicycle and stopped to say hello. We chatted with Pedro who was filming some of the front of venue events, whilst swishing flies away that buzzed around everyone. A guy standing alongside us had already purchased a Crüe tour shirt with the Australian flag on the back. Pedro filmed his back, as there were literally at least fifty flies on him, resting on the Aussie flag. How Australian!

Having been backstage at the venue previously, I knew it would be cramped inside. It was so cramped that as we walked down Campbell Avenue – the side street leading us to the backstage entry – the band's road-cases were stacked along the wide pedestrian footpath. The guys in support band Airbourne were in the back of a truck, setting themselves up for their thirty-minute slot from 8pm. I yakked with the guys and wished them all the best for their set, as Mighty Mike cruised around on his yellow unicycle.

I went backstage to see which dressing rooms the guys were in, before taking Sara in, along with Vicky and Shinbone as he had something to give Nikki. We were in Nikki's dressing room for a while looking at the photos of us from backstage the previous night that he got developed during the day. He gave me a copy of them on CD that he had entitled Friends with a black sharpie.

He also showed us photos on his laptop that he had taken at a Melbourne cemetery and some others of a homeless man on the streets that he stopped and tried to help with some words of encouragement and assistance. Tommy came into Nikki's dressing room and I introduced him to Sara, as he enjoyed looking at some of Nikki's pictures with us.

Nikki then said he needed to have a short meeting so he said to come back in five minutes. We wandered around for a while yakking with friends outside and then Sara and I went back inside and down to catering. Dining on a nice buffet selection, we talked with some of the crew about the Pavlova they were eating for desert, telling them and Mighty Mike that it was probably the most famous Australian desert.

When we came out again, Shinbone was keen to try and head backstage once more, as he hadn't given Nikki his gift. I quickly escorted him back to Nikki's dressing room where he gave Nikki a couple of items that were appreciated.

I had a chat with Jozie who was talking with someone about Tommy's hair and she asked me if I liked the Mohawk she had shaved on him the other day. She said she was keen to party after the show and asked me where I was going afterwards. Knowing that she was an AC/DC fan of course, I suggested she should come with us to Cherry bar in the city, especially since it is in AC/DC Lane (one of only two streets in the world named after the band, the other being in Spain). She was ready to rock with us later in the night.

Told many months ago that there would be no free tickets to this show, Sara and I bought house tickets from the promoter and had our third row centre tickets ready. When we collected a VIP pass for Sara at the ticket window, there were a couple of additional complimentary tickets in the envelope. I rang our friends Angela Fielder and Clea Freeland, who raced to the venue in time to enjoy the show.

Expecting an even more scaled back show tonight, it was great looking around the exquisite 'Spanish Moroccan' interior of the theatre and up to the balcony. When the show kicked off, it was a surprise to see the flame pots and other pyro in use. The smaller stage gave the show a different vibe and it was great to get another perspective on the production from such close proximity.

Nikki dedicated Red Hot "to that motherfucker Shinbone" tonight, which I knew would have thrilled him to bits. The band ripped through Sick Love Song that was omitted from the previous night's Melbourne show. Tommy threw a drumstick out high into the theatre and it was magnificently caught by a guy in the front row… of the balcony. During one song I almost caught a pick thrown out by Vince Neil but lost it in the lights at the last moment. I looked down and saw it sitting on the floor between my feet. Sweet.

As the encore of Anarchy In The U.K. approached, Sara was fearful that she'd be covered in blood. She was pleased she evaded it all, only to get her fair share of the more harmless water pistol squirts to the face instead.

My Mum called my mobile phone during the show's intermission, which caused me some concern, as she never calls my mobile. I called her back after the show, worried that my Dad's health had perhaps taken a bad turn but she was calling to tell me that there were Mötley articles about me published in Perth's newspapers. The heading read, "Mötley Crüe's biggest fan gets to live his rock 'n' roll dream."

Feeling somewhat relieved and pleased it was good news, she continued on telling me how a fan had read the article then got their phone number out of the directory and was asking for information about when the band's flight would arrive in Perth because HE was actually their biggest fan. He said had been calling radio stations trying to find out but they wouldn't tell him. My mum was saying he seemed like a nice person and knowing I would be on the same flight as the band, she wanted to know when I would be in so she could call him back to let him know. I told her that any such information like that can't be given out for security reasons but I got the impression she didn't really grasp what I was saying. I didn't recall my flight details at that moment anyway, so I told her that I will just give her a call when I arrive in Perth and that would be best and to not worry about calling the guy back.

We met back up with Shinbone who was certainly thrilled at Nikki's song dedication to him, commenting to me, "Now I'm on your level." My best reply was silence.

Knowing how cramped and crowded it was backstage, I left everyone else behind and popped back to see if Nikki was going to head out anywhere or just retire to his hotel again. The hotel was the go.

I saw Jozie and we arranged to meet her in the lobby of her hotel so we could go to Cherry bar. Tommy then squished past me in the corridor as he was leaving and said to me that he'll see me at The Loft where he was to be DJing. Not sure what was best to do, Sara and I soon got in a taxi and headed for the Crown hotel to meet Jozie as promised.

We arrived before her and when she came through the lobby she said she'd just be a little while in removing her stage makeup. So we waited a few minutes before she came down again, stage make still intact and eager to just get rocking. We flagged a taxi and took the short drive into the city to AC/DC Lane. We took photos underneath the street sign before venturing into the club.

We grabbed some drinks and headed to the dance floor area as it was the least crowded section of the club. Jozie was immediately rocking out, enjoying the selection of hard rock songs much more than she would have enjoyed Tommy's dance beats. I organised a red Cherry bar t-shirt for her with the owner Bill, as we drank, sang along, and had a great time. Jozie enjoyed watching some of Melbourne's young rockers playing air guitar and jumping around on the dance floor and empty stage, having a blast.

More of our friends arrived in time and soon there was quite a crowd of people that knew each other and were socialising. The Motörhead guys flew on to Adelaide; Bobby O enjoyed drinking and yakking with locals at the bar again.

With everyone having a good time, I felt it was time to walk a few blocks down the city streets to check out Tommy Lee doing his DJ thing. With his set scheduled from midnight to 2am, I knew if I left now I would catch the last half an hour; perfect timing. I asked Crüehead Geoff if he wanted to join me but he decided against, as he would have to start driving to Adelaide in a few hours to make it there in time for the show tomorrow night.

I left Sara dancing with Jozie and headed out the lane on my way. As I neared the top of the street, Geoff yelled out to me and caught up. He said he didn't want to miss it as he would always regret it - wise choice. After all, even though the music is not my cup of tea, it's certainly not every night you can walk to a club and see Tommy Lee performing.

As we walked through the cool night air, I handed Geoff my spare VIP pass and told him that it should get him in for free if he followed behind me at the entrance since I have an All Access one. It did, and he kept the VIP pass as a keepsake.

We made our way through the still-crowded club towards the DJ booth, standing amongst the crowd and taking it all in. One beat turned into another as people danced, swayed and shook their hands in the air to the pounding rhythms. I saw people taking photos so I likewise took advantage of the opportunity to snap some shots of Tommy Lee and his tattooed torso as he grooved along to the sounds that he and his regular turntablist DJ Aero (real name Chester Deitz) were creating.

I wandered off from Geoff after a while and thought I'd say hello to Alecia, Mighty Mike and Pedro in the DJ booth area. Mike was decked out in his superhero costume that was soaked in sweat from his night's work of crowd entertainment. He cheerfully poured shots of Jagermeister into the mouths of willing participants, as Pedro captured all the action with his trusty professional cameras.

Standing behind Tommy in the DJ booth, I got to have a good look at the equipment he was using and how he was cueing and twisting the knobs to keep the beats flowing. I also managed to get some great photos of him in action for myself. At one point he turned around and gave me a high-five when he realised I was standing behind him. He had his laptop sitting on top of a carton of Corona and a keyboard on a carton of Becks.

I made my way back out in the crowd to Geoff as Tommy's set drew to a close at 2:30am and a female DJ took over. We enjoyed the brisk walk back to Cherry bar with Jason and Colin in tow, pleased that we took hold of our opportunities and had another positive Mötley experience to add to our collection.

Arriving back at Cherry, we saw the party was still rocking strong and Ron was telling me how turned on he was at the sight of Jozie dancing in such a raunchy manner with his wife Leah on the dance floor. We kept the drinking and dancing flowing until stumps once more before saying goodbye to everyone after a fantastic night. Jozie headed off with Airbourne's drummer Ryan O'Keefe while Sara and I jumped in a taxi for our ride home.

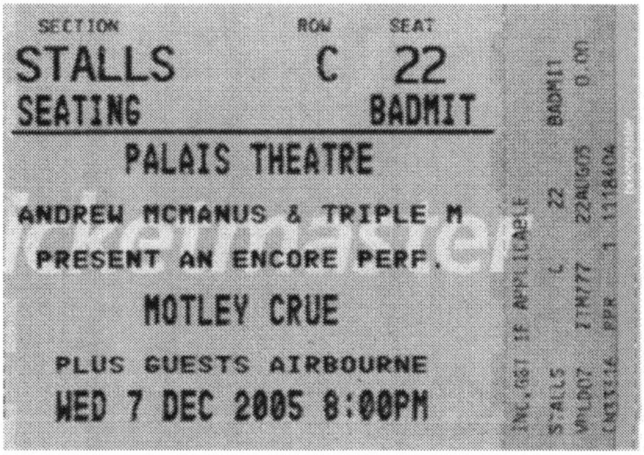
SECTION ROW SEAT
STALLS C 22
SEATING BADMIT
PALAIS THEATRE
ANDREW MCMANUS & TRIPLE M
PRESENT AN ENCORE PERF.
MOTLEY CRUE
PLUS GUESTS AIRBOURNE
WED 7 DEC 2005 8:00PM

CARNIVAL OF SINS
MÖTLEY CRÜE
VIP
7 DEC 05 MLZ

MÖTLEY CRÜE

Wednesday, Dec 7, 2005

PALAIS THEATRE
MELBOURNE, AUSTRALIA

Sound Check: TBA

DINNER: 5:00 pm
DOORS: 7:30 pm

AIRBOURNE 8:00 – 8:30 PM

MÖTLEY CRÜE 9:00

Curfew – 11:0[illegible] pm

AFTERSHOW TRAVEL

RETURN TO MELBOURNE HOTEL
FLY TO ADELAIDE IN THE MORNING

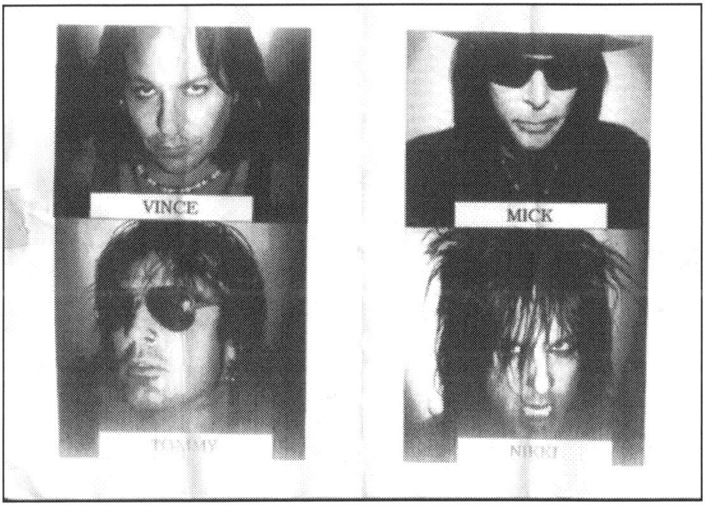
VINCE
MICK
TOMMY
NIKKI

EXIT

ACDC Lane
DURAN DUR
LIVE FROM LONDON

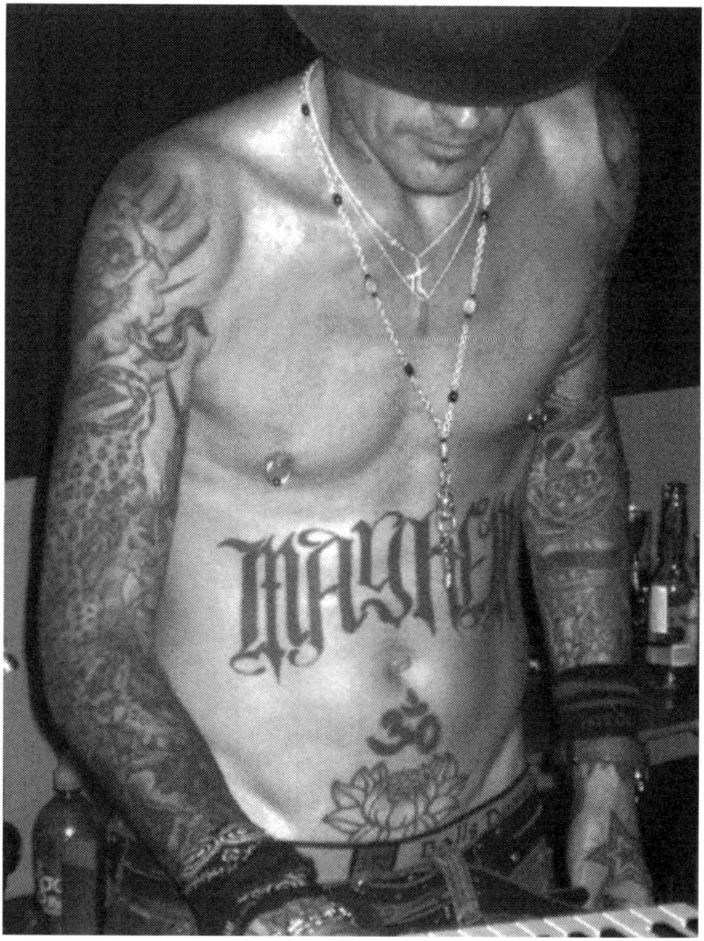

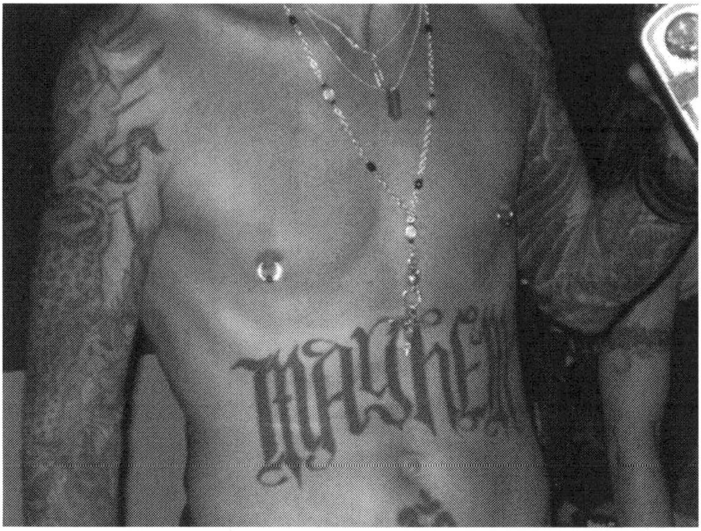

Technics

Thursday, December 8, 2005 - Melbourne to Adelaide

Our alarm went off and I was slow to wake, feeling like I'd only just got to sleep. It was late morning and I needed to pack my bag again and get to the airport for my 1:40 pm flight to Adelaide. As time ticked away while I sluggishly got ready, Sara was telling me that I was going to miss my flight. I finally made it to the airport and checked-in, arriving at the gate's lounge area five minutes before it opened for boarding. I sent Sara a text to let her know everything was fine.

With no sign of the band at the gate, I knew they would be in the Qantas Club lounge. I chatted with a Crüehead Abby Ingleson and her friend briefly before I got a bottle of water to try and relieve my parched throat. Boarding the plane, I made my way to my seat in row 20. The Mötley guys got on last and therefore got off first when we landed in Adelaide shortly after 2:30pm.

Keen to catch up to them as we got off the plane, I left via the rear exit steps down from the aeroplane while the band members exited through the front door. As I stepped onto the tarmac and started walking across, I saw the four band members getting into the four vehicles that were lined up on the tarmac at the front of the plane. A newspaper report later wrote that Nikki was refusing to get into his car because it was the last in the line of four – bullshit.

Patrick said the other vehicles for the crew were through the arrivals lounge and out the front, so I followed through and caught up with Mighty Mike. I yakked with him and Pedro outside for a while. As Chris came through and the van pulled up, he said it was a five-seater and there was no room for me to ride, so I caught a taxi to the hotel instead.

As I checked-in to the Hyatt Regency on North Terrace, I soon saw friends Dean and Rick having a drink in the bar. I said hello to them and some other guys from Perth that I knew: John, Nik and Paul. Inviting me for a drink, I said that I wanted to head up to my room first and drop off my bag. Dean and Rick would be sharing the room with me so they came up with Dean's friend Deb. With sleeping arrangements and keys organised, we headed back down to the bar for a few drinks. My first Scotch & Dry went down fast.

With Dean and Rick able to hang together, I was determined to get to the Entertainment Centre early and just wander around wherever I felt like going. Dean and Rick were heading back to Deb's place to get ready for the show, so they gave me a ride to the venue in her coupe.

I made my way inside and watched a bit of The Casanovas running through their soundcheck. I really dig their classic Australian hard rock sound and they are all great guys to boot. I grabbed a Coke from catering and headed around the corridors to the band dressing rooms. Rhyno and Tam greeted me as they stood outside Mick's door, as usual. They would always be around the corridors and it was always good being around them.

Basia came over and introduced herself, saying she was hired by Fanfire to run the Meet and Greets as part of the Platinum ticket packages. I had a pretty good handle on what her role was but did not tell her that I knew a lot of fans were disappointed with the way their experience had been handled, knowing that the lack of communication was probably not directly attributable to her, even though she was representing the company. Besides, I'm sure a lot of the fans were providing that feedback first hand, and she seemed like a nice person to me. Basia said I should come along to the Meet and Greet to check it out, to which I obliged. After all, this is why I wanted to be at the venues as early as possible, to make the most of any opportunities like this.

Once the band members and their minders all congregated in the corridor, we walked through into the room where the twenty fans were seated. They gave a cheer upon the band's arrival. I stood out of the way with Tam along a wall, making sure I could see the band members lined up against another wall, but not interfering with their experience.

There were a few familiar faces in the fan group. Geoff was there with a big smile on his face. He said he had a great night last night at The Loft and Cherry bar and ended up driving to Adelaide having not gone to sleep at all. I also saw a Crüehead friend Anthony Pitt who had flown in from Tasmania.

It was great to be watching such fans of the band share in a moment they will always treasure, being able to say a couple of words to each band member, get something signed by them and have a couple of pictures snapped with their heroes. As the Platinum fans were lead out, a second group of ten or so contest winners entered. They were quickly filed past the band members before a group photo was taken and they were guided back out the door once more.

I chatted with Nikki and Tommy for a short while once we left the room and waited on some stairs, before heading back through the corridors to the dressing rooms. Having not seen any of The Casanovas' sets to date, I was keen to see them play a couple of songs so I headed out onto the arena's floor and watched them from the side of stage. The guys sounded great as they played their song 10 Outta 10 to the crowd that was steadily building.

It was cool to finally be on my own at the venue nice and early and just wander where I liked, taking snaps as I went. I yakked with Rhyno and Tam in the corridor some more, as Jozie was walking around with her video camera. Tam was giving Rhyno a massage of his shoulders, neck and head. With eyes closed, the expressions on Rhyno's face indicated he was enjoying benefiting from the manipulation from Tam's very strong hands.

Dinner was next on the agenda so I got a feed at catering, leaving in time to walk back out into the auditorium and catch most of Motörhead's set, taking some photos from the side of stage.

Pedro and I chatted about his filming for the night and whether I would take some footage on one of his cameras for him. He offered to set up a camera at the rear of the venue on a tripod for me to film with. However, having to stay with it in position during the entire set, I decided against it, preferring to be closer to the action on stage.

I hung with Nikki's bass tech Darron Meeks for a while as he prepared Nikki's rig and tuned his bass guitars for the show, taking some close-ups of Nikki's basses sitting in their rack and Darron tuning them up as the powerful sounds of Motörhead filled our ears. Half-dressed for the show, Jozie stood on the side of the stage in her pink slippers and filmed Lemmy and Co. ripping through a number or two.

As the crowd gave Motörhead the send off they deserved at the end of their set, I ventured back towards the dressing rooms. Mighty Mike was in his clown outfit walking towards the stage to commence the show. I didn't realise the colours in his costume were quite so vivid, having only seen him wearing it under the stage lights. I snapped some shots of him walking with the costume's head and large gloves in his arms.

The layout of the dressing rooms at this venue had Motörhead's right across from Mötley's. As I approached that area, I spotted Mikkey Dee with a white towel wrapped around his head. Lemmy had also showered and yet to put a shirt on, he was towel-drying his long black hair. At that moment, Nikki came out of his dressing room with a full-face of scary makeup, now ready for the stage. It was the perfect photo opportunity and I snapped an impressive shot of Lemmy and Sixx together.

They exchanged some banter for a short while and before long the rest of the Mötley band members were ready for the show. I followed the performers all the way through to the stage's on-ramp, snapping Rhyno walking Mick up the ramp, who was concentrating too hard to flash any hand signs. I then walked around behind the stage back to Darron's base on Nikki's side of the stage.

As usual, the show got off to a great start. I would never get sick of hearing Shout At The Devil, watching the engaging flames, and feeling their heat mixed with the energy of the crowd's anticipation coming to fruition. It's a brutal opening.

As the band played On With The Show just a few songs into their set, the sound blew out and they had to stop the show while technicians tried to rectify it. Of course it wasn't the actual band's fault and while some of the crowd got agitated, most held their breaths hoping the show could in fact go on. The problem was soon resolved and the Crüe were rocking us once more.

During the ten-minute intermission, I wandered around the back of the stage, curious to see what the band members did during this break. I could see Tommy Lee sitting in a small dressing room tent on the rear of the stage, talking with some of the dancers. Walking around the opposite side of the stage I came across Bobby O's workspace. Mick sat on a stool and chatted with Bobby before he came to the side and said hello to me. I asked Bobby if I could get a shot of him and Mick but Bobby said Mick would prefer just to chill at the moment. We talked a little more before I headed off to catering to grab a drink so I could be back in time for the show re-convening with Girls, Girls, Girls.

Instead of playing Anarchy In The U.K. for the encore, Nikki told the crowd it was the anniversary of John Lennon's death and they hoped he was listening as they ripped into Helter Skelter. I've always loved the way Mötley plays it so it was a nice treat.

Although fairly small in numbers, the Adelaide crowd was enthusiastic and quite loud. I wandered backstage once the show came to a close and yakked with a few of the crew to see if they were kicking on anywhere, since I didn't know the city and its night scene. The casino next to the Hyatt was an option and the strip club across the road that Lemmy enjoyed drinking in the previous night was perhaps another option, but it seemed most people were just going to hit the bar in the hotel's lobby first.

I got a copy of Motörhead's set-list from the night from a lovely German lady who works for their record label SPV and was touring with them. She said she also traveled with Tommy Lee recently in London as his Tommyland: The Ride album is on their label throughout Europe. I promised I would exchange the favour and get her a Mötley set-list before the tour was over.

Kimo and I had a yak outside Nikki's dressing room while he showered. When we went inside, Nikki said hello and walked over to his wardrobe road-case. He pulled out a leather jacket from it and asked if I thought it would fit me. I said I wasn't sure, so he said to try it on. As soon as I put it on he started saying, "Oh, that's perfect!" I said it was a cool jacket and he said I could have it. "No way," I said. Nikki said it was made for him but something about it just doesn't fit him right so I can have it. I asked if he was sure and he said he was. I looked at it in the light-bulb-framed mirror, noting the huge Maltese cross and skull on the back with big lettering underneath spelling out SIXX. Cool.

I spotted Nikki's military-style stage hat sitting on top of the couch, so I picked it up and asked if it was cool if I tried it on. After putting it on, Kimo walked over and pulled it down over my eyes a touch more and said, "There, that's it bro. Killer!" Nikki agreed and then grabbed his cameras to start taking photos of me. He had his crazy Lomographic four-shot one and told me to face my back to him and when he says so, I should spin around fast and give him the devil's horns. Cool photo. I pulled my camera out and asked Kimo to take a shot of Nikki and me. I then took the hat off and left the jacket on as I was getting cold anyway in just my black t-shirt.

It was time to split from the venue so Kimo made one last peanut butter and jelly sandwich. I laughed and told him that was so American and I had to take a photo of him doing that. As Nikki was gathering his belongings he handed me his Qantas boarding pass for business class seat 1F from earlier in the day and said I could have it as a souvenir if I wanted. Sure. It was strange to see "Mr. Nikki Sixx" written on it.

We left the backstage area through the loading bay of the arena and I got into the back of the black Statesman Caprice with Nikki. As we drove out the gate, fans flashed their cameras through the window and Nikki held up a peace sign with his hand. We talked about the show on the way back to the hotel and the different elements of the production. (I forgot to ask what caused the problem with the sound.)

Arriving back at the hotel, we entered via the service area to avoid the foyer and lobby. Vince's car arrived at the same time so we headed through the bowels of the hotel to the elevators. Nikki, Kimo and I caught the lift up with Vince and a girl who was heavily intoxicated. The girl got out on one floor, Nikki and Kimo then missed their stop as we chatted, Vince got out on his floor, then I said goodbye and got out before it went back down to Nikki and Kimo's floor.

I went to my room and got a good look at Nikki's leather jacket that was now mine. I called Dean to let him know I was back at the hotel and he was just about to leave the venue with Rick, so I said I'd meet him in the bar on ground level.

It was the first time that Motörhead, Mötley and their crews were in the same hotel together. So without much else to do in Adelaide, it seemed the best spot for the night was the lobby bar of the hotel, which suited me just fine.

As the night progressed, more and more of the touring party (except the Mötley band members themselves) drank and exchanged conversation amongst themselves and other fans staying at the hotel. It turned into a great party!

A few people were drinking tumblers with crushed lime and mint in the alcohol. I don't recall the name of the cocktail but Kimo was damn sure he started the craze, as everyone seemed to loosen up and enjoy some fun times.

I spotted Lemmy approaching the bar in the wee small hours but seeing the crowd; he turned around and headed back out. The drinks kept flowing until Dean, Rick and I headed back up to our room when the bar closed at 4am. By that time I had had enough Scotch & Dry.

CARNIVAL OF SINS
MÖTLEY CRÜE
VIP

ENTERTAINMENT CENTRE
Andrew McManus & ChV
Present
MOTLEY CRUE
+ guests MOTORHEAD
THU 8 DEC 2005 6:45PM
E B 65
DOOR 4
* COMPLIMENTARY *
* NOT FOR SALE *
COMP
E/B/65
COMP
E
B/65

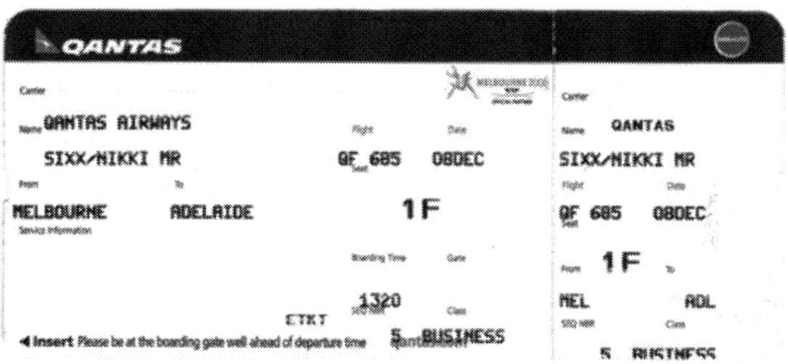
QANTAS
QANTAS AIRWAYS
SIXX/NIKKI MR
QF 685
08DEC
MELBOURNE
ADELAIDE
1F
1320
ETKT
Insert Please be at the boarding gate well ahead of departure time
5 BUSINESS
QANTAS
SIXX/NIKKI MR
QF 685 08DEC
1F
MEL
ADL
5 BUSINESS

MOTORHEAD
SPI

DR. ROCK
STAY CLEAN
LOVE ME LIKE A REPTILE
KILLERS
METROPOLIS
OVER THE TOP
NO CLASS
I GOT MINE
TRAGEDY
DANCING ON YOUR GRAVE
FAST AND LOOSE
RAMONES
SACRIFICE
POWER
BRAZIL
KILLED BY DEATH
IRON FIST

WHORE HOUSE BLUES
ACE OF SPADES
OVERKILL

MÖTLEY CRÜ

CATERING

ADELAIDE
SHOUT
TOO FAST
10 SECONDS
RED HOT
ON WITH SHOW
LOOKS KILL
LOUDER HELL
LIVE WIRE
GIRLS
WILD SIDE
DON'T GO
PRIMAL
GLITTER
WITHOUT YOU
HOME SWEET
FEELGOOD
SOS
KICKSTART
ANARCHY
B
G
E
G

mötley crüe ✠ nikki sixx

Friday, December 9, 2005 - Adelaide to Perth

As we awoke to the sounds of the alarm clock, Dean, Rick and I slowly stirred and began chatting about the events of the previous night before getting ready to check out. They were staying another day in Adelaide and were going to a BBQ at a Rose Tattoo member's place. I had time to kill before my 4:45pm flight to Perth, so I stored my bag with hotel concierge, rather than taking it with me on a walk around the city.

I saw the Perth fans checking out of their room and chatting with them they showed me a newspaper review of last night's show. "Boo, hiss as Crüe blows it" read the headline of the typically negative article that started, "There was almost a real rock'n'roll riot at the Entertainment Centre last night..." Reception made me a photocopy of the piece of junk journalism that I folded into my pocket as I walked out. Another critic that failed to make it as an artist, I'm sure.

I'd never spent time in Adelaide before so I was keen to check out the streets a bit. I was surprised that the tallest buildings in the city seemed only about as tall as the Melbourne apartment I live in. I strolled through the long mall and targeted an appetising café for my dose of bacon and eggs for brunch.

Nothing was really exciting me, and the shops felt kind of bland. I stopped in a bong shop and checked out their rock t-shirts and other merchandise. There was one cool AC/DC logo patch left so I bought it and continued on my way. I phoned home and had a good catch-up with Sara for an hour or so, which felt like a better use of my time.

Walking back into the hotel lobby, I saw Anthony from Tasmania, so I had a good chat with him for a while, as various members of the crew were arriving for lobby call. Chris came by and I asked if he thought he'd have room in the people mover for me this trip. Matter-of-factly, he said it would only be a five-seater again so I'd have to make my own way there.

Kimo soon approached and said to me, "Bro, I am so fucking pissed off right now. These hotel idiots broke my luggage handle and now they are trying to tell me that it was already broken when I was standing in front of them when he busted it." Hot under the collar, Kimo was negotiating the situation with the hotel staff. "I am not a stupid man. I was standing there when he broke it and you are trying to tell me that it didn't happen. I am not a fool," he continued to them.

I tried to calm him a bit and said they'll surely sort it out in the correct manner for you. Kimo said they had to leave and were already running behind schedule. Somewhat reluctantly but taking the chance anyway, I asked him if I could perhaps grab a ride with him and Nikki to the airport since there was no room for me in the other vehicles. He said he'd check with Nikki as he went back up to his room to sort his luggage situation further with the staff.

Talking with Anthony, I soon heard a whistle, turning around to see Kimo at the bottom of the lifts giving me a come on signal with his hand. I said goodbye and hopped in the elevator with Kimo. He said that Nikki said it's cool but he's not happy. Hoping it wasn't because of me in any way, I asked why and he said it was because they were behind schedule thanks to the poor hotel treatment. When I asked if they ended up sorting out his luggage handle situation, Kimo said they promised to have it resolved by the time he left the Hyatt in Perth, as he had no more time to deal with it now.

Kimo and I went through the service area of the hotel again and I quickly got into the back of the black Statesman where Nikki was sitting, placing my hand-luggage bag between my feet. I thanked him for the ride and he seemed like normal Nikki to me, so I felt more comfortable than I thought I would.

As we drove to Adelaide Airport, Nikki pulled some of his funky cameras out of his bag and was showing them to me. He had an interesting Lomography Oktomat 35mm camera that, with one touch of the shutter button, has eight tiny lenses that fire in turn over two seconds, creating an arty, multi-frame, mini-photo vignette on each print. It looked like a kid's plastic toy camera.

I then reached into my bag and showed him my new little digital recorder and asked him to perhaps say a little message that I could put on the Chronological Crue website. He obliged and said the recorder was a pretty cool little tool.

I told him that I had the guitar strap from the smashed bass that he gave me in my hand luggage and that I wouldn't mind having him sign it. He said that was no worries but it was probably best to wait until we got to the airport where he can have a hard surface to write on.

Pulling up at the airport we were met by fans seeking autographs and wanting photos taken. I was now getting used to it being around me and while it is cool, I can certainly understand how it would become annoying for celebrities who are faced with it constantly for years, not just around it for a week like the taste I was experiencing.

Nikki stopped for a smoke before entering the terminal, spending some time with fans by signing items, including a red car boot (trunk) lid with Mötley Crüe emblazoned on it that one guy was lugging around. I gave Kimo a hand with some luggage from the boot and we checked-in. Kimo was stopped by the x-ray security as he had what looked to be a small pair of metal pliers or clippers in his hand luggage. This added to his stress as Nikki had already gone through and was walking through the airport with fans circling him. I waited with Kimo for a while to see if he wanted me to do anything to assist him, before taking one of Nikki's camera bags and catching up to him.

As we entered the Qantas Club lounge, we saw the rest of the touring party already working their way through soup, fruit and drinks. An annoyed Kimo soon joined us; his day had got off to a bad start but hopefully it was to only improve from here. I got a Corona and sat with Rhyno, Tam and Mick. The slouching Mars man was again lightening my mood with some wisecracks.

I spoke with Nikki to plan our intentions to visit Bon Scott's grave once we got to Perth, telling him tonight would be our best opportunity but we'd have to move quick before the sun sets since we were due to arrive at 5:35pm and there was no daylight savings in Perth. With a thirty-minute drive required to reach the cemetery in Fremantle, Nikki said it would be best to go straight from the airport instead of heading to the hotel first. I agreed and told Jozie the plan, who replied, "Make sure you don't leave without me!"

My friend and former band-mate Stevie D was going to meet me at the airport, since I was going to spend the night at his place. As I drank the last of my beer in the lounge, I called him and said I'd give him another call once I was back at the city hotel and we could meet up then instead.

We boarded 'Dysfunction Junction Airlines' and it was a slightly smaller aircraft than the previous ones. Mick and Lemmy occupied seats in the first row with Vince and Nikki sitting two rows behind. Tommy was also in the third row across the aisle and I sat another two rows behind Tommy in the fifth. This plane had no petitions between the business class and economy seats, so I was able to observe as a fly on the wall.

Tommy was looking to nap right away, constantly adjusting his Billabong fedora hat over his eyes trying to get comfortable for a snooze. Mick and Lemmy chatted most of the flight, as Lemmy also flicked through the latest issue of Rolling Stone magazine. Vince sat still in his seat the whole flight, chatting occasionally with Nikki and drinking white wine the whole flight, spilling a glass-full on his seat in the process. The lady behind Nikki tried to work on her laptop and sighed every time Nikki would shuffle in his seat. One would think Nikki was drinking the wine because he went to the toilet cubicle about ten times during the flight.

Tommy later woke up and drank some miniature bottles of vodka. I showed him the photocopied review from the previous night and he just shook his head as he passed it back over the seat to me. A couple of middle-aged passengers approached Tommy and Nikki for autographs during the flight, to which they obliged.

As we started our descent into Perth, a concert of Fremantle band John Butler Trio aired on the monitors. Lemmy put his headphones on and nodded along to some tracks, passing them to give Mick a listen from time to time. Tommy also tuned in for a listen and seemingly liked what he heard as he watched the screen.

Landing in Perth, we disembarked the plane and I thought I'd probably see some of my friends and former band-mates in the arrivals area. However the Crüe had again arranged for a tarmac transfer so I took a side door with Tommy and headed down the stairs onto the bitumen where the chauffeurs and their cars were lined up and ready to roll.

I told Tommy that I had recently been emailing with his first wife, Elaine Starchuk (aka Candice Starrek), and that she had a message to pass on to him. As I did my best to recall the right context of her message, Tommy said he had heard recently that she had died. He asked if I was sure if it was her and I answered that I was certain and said that I would email him the full message from her once I got back home. He said thanks.

I then got into the last black Statesman in the line with Nikki as we waited for Jozie. I knew she was sitting further back on the plane and would be a little while longer but I started to get concerned that she may have gone through into the airport terminal. I was relieved when I saw her come down the stairs and onto the tarmac. With Jozie between Nikki and me on the back seat and Kimo in the front, we told the driver that we would not be going to the hotel with the other cars but to Fremantle Cemetery instead. He called through to inform the other drivers in the procession.

Not long after we pulled off the tarmac and out of the airport through a side gate, my mobile phone started beeping with text messages. I had some friends waiting in the airport terminal but all they could do was watch through the glass, disappointed they couldn't say hello and get any signatures or photos. My former guitarist and Crüehead friend Corey Hodgetts rang and said, "I know you are busy now but let's catch up for a drink later" so I said, "Give me an hour and a half or so and I will."

Driving to the graveyard, we talked about AC/DC and how Bon had died. I encouraged Nikki that it would be cool for Mötley to include an AC/DC song as their standard cover song on the band's next studio album. I reminded him that they used to jam a bit on Highway to Hell during the Theatre of Pain days, but perhaps they should do something less obvious. I told him I felt Girls Got Rhythm could work in with the Crüe's vibe, or perhaps even Problem Child. Jozie felt that Problem Child gets covered a lot by bands in the U.S.

My former band SkinInc. had a cover version of Touch Too Much included on an AC/DC Hometown Tribute CD a few years back. Even though I sang it in a lower register than Bon, I told them that it was still a fun song to do that sounded great and Jozie said it was probably her favourite AC/DC track. They thought it was cool as I told them how we used to drive down this very same highway on our way to play gigs in Fremantle and sometimes call in to see Bon on the way before performing the cover in our set of originals later in the night.

I also told them how I was sitting at a friend's place one night with Cam Muncey from Jet and he put on AC/DC's album For Those About To Rock. When the song Night of the Long Knives played from the B-side of the vinyl, we were amazed at how similar the riff was to Dr. Feelgood. Nikki didn't know the song and hadn't heard of that before, so I said I'd have to send him an MP3 of it to check out.

Nikki said he was actually keen for Jet to play as support on this tour but it didn't happen. I told him that I have always thought the Backyard Babies would be a cool support for the Crüe and he said he hasn't heard their stuff. I told him some more about them and encouraged him to check them out.

We talked about the grind of touring and how they could actually be driving through a state of America at the moment and they wouldn't even realise it. While the passing view was foreign to them, I was getting all sorts of flashback memories as we drove past familiar sights from the first thirty years of my life that I spent in Perth. I told them that most of the American sailors that dock into Perth say it's like California, but smaller. Nikki nodded in agreeance, looking out his window.

After our thirty-minute drive, we arrived at Fremantle Cemetery, as the sun was about to fall down behind the surrounding trees. Keen to use the remaining daylight, we swiftly headed for the northwest corner of the grounds at the corner of Leach Highway and Carrington Street. Even though I'd been there before I had a printout map with me as I led them past other plots and headstones, just in case I couldn't recall the exact location.

"There it is," I said as I stopped abruptly. Bon's resting plaque and memorial seat were in front of us. Jozie was filming with her video camera and Nikki and Kimo started taking photos. Since I already had photos of the plaques at home from years ago, I hung back and took photos of them taking photos of the memorials. We checked out all the surrounding graffiti-style messages etched into the kerbing and footpath in front of the plot currently adorned with an Australian flag and a can of VB beer from a past visitor.

Jozie sat in front of the seat with her pink AC/DC t-shirt on; laying her head back onto the seat and feeling as close as should could to Bon. The wind blew her curly, peroxided locks over the plaque, so I moved them to one side to not obscure the writing as Nikki took some snaps of her.

Nikki soon wandered off; his eye caught by some other attractive photo opportunities with the setting sun behind. Kimo was behind him and Jozie and I started off after them until she said, "Wait! That was all a bit quick. I need to just spend a moment." I knew what she meant.

I stood behind her as she said some words that were inaudible to me. With her head bowed, I watched her reflecting, assuming she was thanking Bon for the music, and the attitude, and perhaps what his art means to her. Whatever she was doing and saying, it didn't matter. It was clearly a special moment that she was having. I waited until she was done and walked over to her.

I put my arm around her shoulder and said, "I promised I'd bring you here." She said, "Yes, you did. Thank you so very much Paul." "My pleasure," I said as I reached into my back pocket before continuing, "I got a little something for you." Her eyes lit up as I passed her the little AC/DC logo patch I bought in Adelaide. She hugged me tight, "Dude! That is SO going on my jacket. Thanks heaps."

We then caught up to Kimo and Nikki, who was setting up for an amazing photograph of a cross headstone with an angel in view at its rear, and the bright light of the setting sun behind. We admired the very old and rusted wrought iron bordering on some of the graves and we started to wander back towards the car.

With Nikki and Kimo moving ahead, Jozie remembered that her friend wanted her to get some soil from the site of Bon's grave. Not wanting to hold Nikki up, we decided we'd have to act quickly. After looking around for a container, Jozie grabbed the base of a broken glass jar from next to a grave and we ran the couple of hundred metres towards Bon's location. Jozie was taking video and photos as we laughed and ran through the cemetery together.

After scooping some soil (probably soaked with alcohol) from next to his plaque, we jogged back towards the car. As we turned the corner and the car came into view, we saw a couple of fans nearby saying some words to Nikki and Kimo who were getting in the car. As Jozie and I passed them they called out my name to say hello; I'd never seen them before in my life.

With light fading, we headed back towards the city of Perth, tailed by the fans. I asked Kimo if they said how they knew we were there and he said they must have followed us from the airport. The driver took a small detour that put their car in front of ours where Kimo watched them. Knowing the roads, I told the driver to turn left at the next set of lights and head into the city via Canning Highway to get us off Leach Highway. We lost them.

Nikki talked about the Crüe and how it can be frustrating not knowing how long it all may last, or if it may blow up on any given day. He said that whilst he of course appreciates the fans, he's had to deal with them for so many years now. He talked about just disappearing one day to escape it all. "People will say, you know that fucker Sixx, where the hell did he get to?" The band has played a lot of shows this year and I felt Nikki's batteries were running low.

Jozie said she thought it was great that Nikki had his photography as a creative outlet and something alternative to music to be into and enjoy while on and off the road. Nikki and I agreed and he said it was very cool that he was sharing his love of photography as an interest with his wife Donna.

Nikki said he recently told Donna that he wanted to get an old '60s photo booth for their studio so people can have their photos taken in it when they visit. I said that it reminded me of Dave Navarro's book he did with Neil Strauss.

Driving along the freeway, we spotted the sun out my window, just as it was about to dip below the horizon on the Swan River. We pulled into the emergency lane, stopping to take some shots of it. Kimo could smell the water and asked if it was salt water or fresh water. I told him it was salt water and there would sometimes be some seaweed in this Como Beach area. I told them how I recall coming to this beach as a child with my family. The men would trawl the water with a prawning net at dusk before the women would cook the catch and we'd sit around under the light from lanterns as we shelled them and ate.

Now a little hungry, we considered going somewhere for food, but decided to head back into the hotel instead. Arriving via a private carpark, I asked Nikki if it was OK if I came up to his room for a moment so he could sign my guitar strap. Nikki said sure.

He opened the door of his room 818 and took his shoes off before putting the TV on and flicking channels, leaving it on The Simpsons. I asked if his kids watched The Simpsons and he said, "Of course." I told him that mine grew up on it as well. We yakked for a while as strawberries dipped in chocolate were consumed.

While getting my silver pen out of my bag, I remembered I had brought along a printout of an old email from Nikki that I came across shortly before the tour. I had emailed him a Happy Birthday and his reply email of thanks dated 11 Dec 1995 and talking about his '57 Chevy took up the printout. We both were saying how cool it was that it was now just two days short of a decade that he had sent that to me. It's been a long time that we have been in touch with each other.

I then showed him another piece of paper and asked him if he wouldn't mind signing it. It was the cover page of my Rough Draft copy of *The Dirt* manuscript that Neil Strauss sent me as I worked on the book while it neared completion. Nikki signed it: "Paul – Live long – Your the best. Nikki Sixx." He then unexpectedly wrote across the email printout: "Paul, Its been a very long road. What a trip. Your amazing. With love & respect, Nikki."

We chatted some more about our families and he showed me his beautiful little wooden pinhole camera, pulling it apart to display the very simplistic inner workings. We talked about combining photos and words to create cool things. I told him that I want to make more time next year to write more as I really enjoy it. Nikki said that writing can be difficult for him as his poor schooling rendered him a bad speller. I already knew that.

He then got the silver marker working nicely on the guitar strap that I had lain out and wrote "Paül – Your great – Nikki Sixx" on it. I couldn't help but point out his slight spelling error, so he changed it to "Paül – Your'e great – Nikki Sixx". We laughed.

It turned out that these were the only signatures I got on the tour; it didn't feel right any other time and I was totally comfortable with that. Others had asked me to get some things signed by the band if I could but it just wasn't appropriate. I was sure they would understand; too bad if they couldn't.

Nikki said he was just going to have a lazy day tomorrow and perhaps we could do lunch or something. I said that I wanted to visit my parents as I hadn't seen them for a couple of years and before the show would be my only opportunity. He said his only thing he wanted to do was to get some more film developed and then just hang out and take it easy. I told him I'd catch him at the show tomorrow instead; the last of the tour.

I called my parents and told them that I had landed in Perth fine and that I would come and visit them tomorrow before the show. I then got back to Corey who was down in the hotel's bar, so I said I'd see him in a tick. Spotting Corey in the bar, I said hello and was introduced to his girlfriend, before saying hello to another friend Jason and his brother Mick, who I recalled used to work for the Crüe's record label in Perth during the eighties.

It was good to catch up with Corey again over a couple of drinks and they were keen to hear how the tour was going. Stevie D soon arrived and joined us for another drink before I headed back to his house, picking up a couple of pizzas on the way. We downed the slices with his pregnant wife Mel as we sat around talking and drinking, with the new live Mötley DVD playing in the background.

As the night wore on, I was ready for a good sleep. It had been another eventful day full of memories to keep. Tomorrow was the last concert and I wanted to enjoy my finale. As I closed my eyes for the night, images of the events at the cemetery replaced the darkness in my head. What a day!

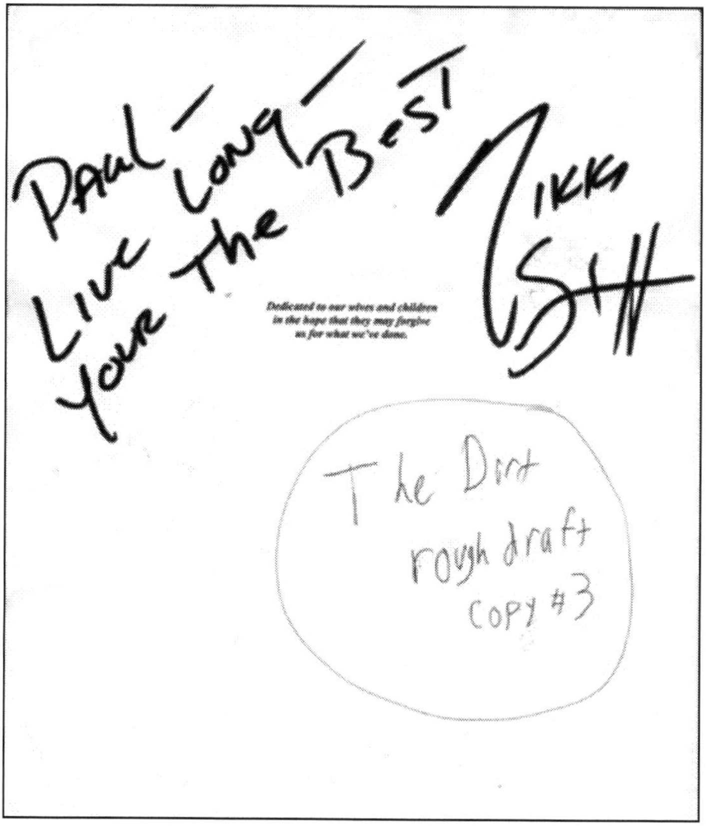
Paul — Live Long — Your the Best
Nikki Sixx
Dedicated to our wives and children
in the hope that they may forgive
us for what we've done.
The Dirt
rough draft
copy #3

SIXXDOG@aol.com, 08:15 11/12/95 -, Re: HAPPY BIRTHDAY

X-POP3-Rcpt: paul@asterix
Return-Path: SIXXDOG@aol.com
From: SIXXDOG@aol.com
Date: Mon, 11 Dec 1995 08:15:32 -0500
To: paul@interworld.com.au
Subject: Re: HAPPY BIRTHDAY

HEY BRO..THANKS...I GOT MY SELF A DREAM MACHINE..VERY CLEAN.....SHES GOT 540
HORSE...AN LOVE TO SUCK....GAOLINE...TONIGHT I TAKE HER OUT AN PLAY WITH HERE
THROTTLE..SHES A 1957 CHEVY.........WHAT SHALL I CALL HER??

Paul, its Been A very Long Road. what A Trip. your Amazing.

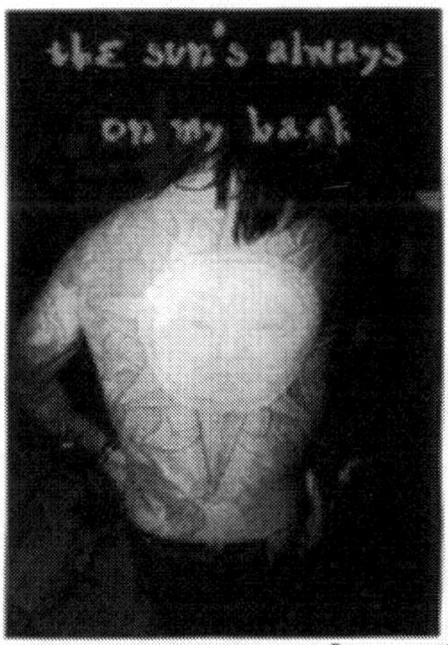

with Love & Respect
Nikki

Printed for Paul Miles <paul@business.com.au>

PAUL—

YOU'RE GREAT!

NIKKI SIXX

Saturday, December 10, 2005 - Perth

We woke up in the morning and went for a ride around the streets on Steve and Mel's scooters. I looked around Carousel shopping centre with Steve and got a little gift for Nikki. Upon return, we tucked into some bacon and eggs that Mel cooked for us before they kindly drove me to my parents' house on the other side of town.

Mum and Dad were pleased to see me of course, as it had been a bit over two years since the last time. My sister and two nieces also came over so we had a good catch-up, with the young ones asking me about the shows, poking and scratching my tattoos to see if they come off and generally having good kiddie fun. Mum gave me the newspaper article that she previously phoned me about. I took a moment to read it:

> **Paul says, 'On with the Show'**
>
> **Motley Crue's biggest fan gets to live his rock 'n' roll dream**
>
> Former Kallaroo resident Paul Miles is arguably US rock outfit Motley Crue's biggest fan. Now based in Melbourne, Miles claims to be the world's number one historian and biographer of the group, having documented the facts behind the band's rock and roll lifestyle since 1995.
>
> Miles was first introduced to the band by his girlfriend more than 15 years ago.
>
> "In my late teens, I was first introduced to the band's first album by a girlfriend and I still love that album heaps and the same with the girl, we have been married for 15 years," he said.
>
> "After that, I began collecting Motley items and exploring the band's history, learning more about them and being amazed by their rock and roll antics."

Miles is so obsessed with the band that in 1994 he launched a dedicated website that has had more than four million hits.

He said he decided to start up a website because when he first logged on to the internet there was little information on his favourite band.

Miles added another notch to his leather Motley Crue belt by tackling the role of executive producer on an award-winning tribute CD. After unsuccessfully pitching to management the idea of turning his history content into a book, Miles was eventually hired in 2001 to assess the manuscript of the band's autobiography *The Dirt.*

"The infamous story is being turned into a big-screen Hollywood movie and I have since given assistance to the movie's screenwriter in verifying the accuracy of the script," he said.

Six years ago the band asked Miles to write the liner notes in their first live album, Live: Entertainment or Death.

"My piece summed up the band's live history from a fan's perspective," he said.

"But the most amazing thing is that until now, I have yet to see a live Motley Crue show."

Fans of the band can thank Miles for his work earlier in the year when he was involved in starting up a petition to bring Motley Crue to Australia.

Miles will be part of the "Crue" and will travel with them on tour, including their show at Claremont Showgrounds on Saturday, December 10.

"The last time I stood on the same turf in Claremont was when I fronted my hard rock band SkinInc. and sang the national anthem before 5000 speedway fans," he said.

After the shows finish, there will be a few new Crue things for Miles to do.

"I am turning my history on the band into a three-volume set of books and am also editing a book of submissions from fans titled What Motley Crue Means to Me, both of which will be published early in 2006," he said.

> Miles will also document his tour adventures and keep up his free newswire service.
>
> "With all the events that have transpired through the years, the prospect of getting to meet all of the band members and finally see them perform live is a dream come true for me."

Mum and Dad thought it was great and were proud. Seeing an article in print, they seemed to finally understand more about what this whole Mötley Crüe thing is, which I've been spending so much time on over the years. I felt it gave them some tangible proof that my pursuits had been worthy to some degree. We continued to chat and they were keen to find out what I had been up to on the tour so far.

Later in the afternoon, and running about an hour behind our schedule, Steve then picked me up with some mates Johnno and Wazza in the car. They handed me a can of Jim Beam and cola and we were on our way to the Blackjack festival.

We parked near Claremont Oval and walked around to the entrance of the Claremont Showgrounds. There was a long line, so I said to Steve that I would go on ahead and see if the tickets were ready, as I had one allocated for him as his entry. They weren't, as I expected, so I went inside and headed behind the stages. There were a couple of production offices there but no-one I could ask about promoter tickets and when they would be ready for collection out the front.

I had a chat with Pedro for a little while who had recently arrived and was upset that some of his photographic equipment, including a cardboard box full of film, had been left in the sun for quite some time. He felt that as the tour wore on, he could see people starting to tire and take short cuts.

I then headed around to the management offices and dressing rooms behind the grandstand to try and sort out the ticket situation. I spoke with Steve on the phone and he had managed to get in to the venue fine, as he knew a guy on the gate, so that relieved the immediate pressure of having him waiting outside.

As I made my way through the various rooms, I stumbled upon the Perth meet and greet for Platinum ticket holders that was just about to get underway, so I stood with Tam again and watched the going-ons as the band entered and met with the fans. Again there were some familiar faces in the group of twenty diehards.

After that I went upstairs to the band dressing rooms, grabbed a Corona out of the tub, and hung with Nikki for a while in his black-walled temporary cubicle. He told me to pull up a chair, so I moved aside his stage clothes that were hanging over the chair and sat with him at his desk.

We talked about what we got up to during the day. He showed me some photos of an Aboriginal woman that he took in Forest Place as he wandered the city, managing to escape Kimo's constant security shadow for a little while.

I said to Nikki that he has now managed to see a bit of most Australian capital cities and wondered which city he perhaps liked best. Without hesitation he replied, "Oh Melbourne." Having enjoyed living there for the last five years myself, I agreed with him whole-heartedly that it was the best.

We continued chatting and I told him a bit about catching up with my family and I showed him my newspaper article. He read it through and said, "I didn't know your wife got you into the Crüe" and I said, "Yep, she sure did." He finished the article and said that he thought it was very cool and said, "Well done man, that's awesome."

I told him that I had some killer shots of him and Lemmy from backstage in Adelaide and some more from our Fremantle grave visit. He asked me to pop out the memory stick from my digital camera and he put it into his laptop to copy all the photos I had taken on the tour. This saved me the trouble of burning them all to CD and posting it to his house once we returned from tour.

Copying the photos, he was renaming the best one as Lemmy & Sixx. When I suggested he should call it Killed By Breath he said, "Oh, fuck yeah! That's killer dude." He then prepared it for upload onto his website, showing me the filters that he uses in Photoshop to create cool borders.

I gave him a little gift of a silver cigarette case as a thank you and happy birthday. He said he nearly bought one the other day but didn't so it was a great gift. He took all the menthols out of his open packet and laid them in his new case. Poking it into his back pocket, he said it was perfect because his smokes wouldn't get crushed anymore.

After a while I said I'd let him do his thing and I went to check out some of The Living End's set. Seeing my good friend Georgia Kennedy, who was queued at the ladies toilet, we had a quick chat as I remembered to head back to the ticket window to see if the tickets had arrived by now. They had and there was an extra one so I called my sister-in-law Emma who quickly caught a train down to the Showgrounds with her boyfriend. I watched some of The Living End's set from the crowd before heading to the backstage lawns behind the two stages. I chatted with Mighty Mike as a wardrobe lady had his clown head laid out ready for some running repairs.

With limited room around the stage, it seemed the best, closest spot to watch the bands from was on the side of the actual stage. So as Motörhead's set began, I walked up onto the 'Ace of Spades' stage and around behind Mikkey Dee and he bashed his drums, taking a few photos on my way. It was awesome standing alongside his kit just twenty feet from him as he flung stick after stick into the air at the end of Killed By Death. I stood alongside Jozie and just fifteen feet across and behind Lemmy as they belted out Ace of Spades followed by Overkill. Born to lose, live to win - It was a magic moment and I was living it.

Right as Motörhead finished their set, the Crüe's performance started on the bigger 'Queens of Hearts' stage next door. I headed up the stairs at the rear of the stage and soon took up position leaning against Sixx's rack of basses, as I watched the show from my closest vantage point of the tour thus far.

The show was awesome once again and it was yet another different perspective on it that I was enjoying. At one point, I laughed at Kimo as he brushed pyro remnants from his cropped hair, and he was wincing at me as the strobe lights played havoc with his eyes during Live Wire.

The Perth crowd was loud. I'm not sure if it was due to my position or not, but I recall thinking that this was probably the loudest crowd I'd heard on the tour. The Fremantle doctor breeze was also blowing in the right direction to carry the audience sound best so perhaps that was also a factor. Regardless, it was good, especially when Nikki chanted, "Aussie, Aussie, Aussie" and the crowd responded with a booming "Oi, Oi, Oi."

With only a ninety-minute set tonight, the band played through without stopping for intermission. Mötley finished Kickstart My Heart and Nikki smashed another bass. This time I watched his lips say "For Lemmy" as he gave it to Kimo to remove from the stage. Awesome.

I saw a Marshall speaker stack with head on top being rolled around backstage a song or two ago. I thought they were clearing out some gear from the support bands until I looked around behind me. Mikkey Dee, Phil Campbell and Lemmy were all standing right behind me watching the show. Mikkey then said hello to me and told me that they were going to jam on the encore song.

With the stage in darkness as roadies started getting a couple of new rigs for Lemmy and Phil into position, Vince Neil walked around behind me. He started talking to Lemmy about how they were going to sing Anarchy in the U.K. Lemmy was saying he didn't really know the words, so Vince said he should sing the second verse because no-one cares about second verses anyway. They were both laughing and Vince started running through the lyrics out loud for Lemmy. I snapped a photo of them together discussing it, in fact it was the only photo I took of Vince for the entire tour – quality, not quantity.

With the song about to commence, lots of members of the touring party crept even closer to the performance area of the stage to get good vantage points with digital cameras and video cameras. I captured some video footage on my digital camera. Lemmy was out front playing bass and singing the chorus with Vince, who had his arm around Lemmy. Phil Campbell was wandering the stage with Nikki, as Mighty Mike, Jozie, Brandy and Alecia played with fire and danced around them. In line with the drum kit, Mikkey Dee was in the driver's seat of Tommy Lee's kit while Tommy stood behind him belting out another rhythm.

I thought to myself that this may be the last time I see Mötley Crüe perform a song live on stage, a stage that I was also standing on nonetheless. And even if I did see them play again, this was certainly a great moment in rock and a fitting way to end the tour and one of the best weeks of my life. I soaked it up best I could.

As the song and the show drew to a close, the members of both bands and performers exited the stage, as roadies started to gather their equipment. I returned the set-list favour by asking Darron if I could have the Mötley one for Unther. He said sure and handed it to me. I was about to ask if I could have a couple of Nikki's picks from the two bags of them on his work area but he had swung into busy action heading across the stage. Trusting he wouldn't mind, I grabbed a couple of picks and headed down onto the backstage lawn area, watching the Crüe and Motörhead get into the vehicles to head back around the other side of the oval.

I yakked with Pedro and Mighty Mike for a while before I walked back across the emptying oval that was littered with evidence of a great time. Arriving back at the dressing rooms, I saw all the Mötley band members milling around a hospitality area with food, drink and trestle tables, as they chatted with members of the touring party. Lemmy was also there.

As I joined them, Vince was heading off past me so I said a quick goodbye to him and his security guy Ray as Nikki was telling Vince that he'd see him in Hawaii. I chatted with Jozie about how cool that encore was and that it was great that she got to perform on stage with Lemmy. She loved the moment too. That said, the man was right behind me talking with Tommy Lee, so I asked Jozie if she could grab a photo of Lemmy and I.

As she photographed us, I started to pick a bone with Lemmy, telling him that he used to keep my wife awake at night. He looked at me a little puzzled before I explained. Her mum used to live in a squat on Burnt Ash Hill in South-East London, occupying an upper floor. A band used to frequently jam in her basement, often waking up my wife Sara as she was about four years old. Her mum used to go downstairs and yell at them to turn it down. It was Lemmy and his band Hawkwind, before the days of Motörhead. Lemmy said he didn't recall Burnt Ash Hill and thought it may have been before he joined the band, but lining all the dates up we know it was him. Either way, we laughed about it for a little bit.

Just then Basia brought out a birthday cake for Nikki, with twenty candles and "Happy Birthday Nikki" written across the top of it. Nikki was telling people he was twenty-five but I knew it was his 47th being celebrated. Everyone gathered around and sang Happy Birthday to Nikki before he blew out the candles in a single blow.

With the candles now extinguished, Mick Mars was ready to head off with Rhyno and Tam. After one last flash of our gouging hand sign, I said goodbye and thank you to Mick, before Tam or Rhyno took our photo. I gave them both a hug goodbye and was sad to see them go. I had enjoyed our many chats together outside Mick's dressing room door, in Qantas Club lounge tub chairs and during band Meet and Greets. I told them both to make sure they give me a yell if ever they come to Melbourne again, and I would do likewise if I were in their cities.

As I moved back over towards the main table, I saw Nikki cutting his birthday cake, handing out pieces on plates to Lemmy, Tommy, and others. I took some photos with Jozie while waiting for everyone to get a piece. There was plenty left so I couldn't resist tasting some. As I ate the delicious choc-topped sponge with a thin layer of jam and thick layer of custard cream in the middle, I thought about the last backstage cake for Tony that turned into a food fight and hoped that the events didn't repeat. They didn't thankfully.

I walked past Jozie on the way to the drinks tub and I put out my open hand to give her a high-five. She stopped and she grabbed my hand instead. Looking at it, she said, "Wow. You have beautiful hands." Curious, I asked why she thought and said that. She told me that I must be a very creative person because I certainly have the hands of an artist. "Interesting", I said as I got my drink and mingled some more.

Brandy soon came up and said goodbye and we exchanged contact details. It was a shame I had to say goodbye to my new friends. I gave Jozie a big hug and promised to keep in touch. As she knows, I'm true to my word and keep my promises. We had a huge amount of fun together and shared some special times, none more so than at Bon Scott's grave the previous day.

As Tommy and Mighty Mike left, I told them I'd see them at Tommy's DJ set at Club Capitol on Murray Street in Perth. I stayed a bit longer and chatted with others.

Nikki said he was flying out at lunchtime tomorrow and maybe we could ride to the airport together. Even though our flights were roughly both in the middle of the day, it would be trickier since I wasn't staying at the hotel, and the domestic terminal for my Melbourne flight and the International terminal for his flight to Hong Kong were a different route.

So we decided to leave it at that and promised to catch up with each other again in person as soon as we can. I thanked him for allowing me to share the tour with him and the rest of the party and he said it was awesome to have me around for so long so we could really get to know each other a lot more.

Nikki asked me if I needed a lift. I said that I had some friends waiting for me but I appreciated the offer anyway. With a hug it was sadly goodbye until next time.

I said goodbye to Kimo who gave me one of his (teddy) bear hugs and he said he'd be in touch with me to catch up in

January when he visits Australia next. I walked downstairs with them as they got into their car. I said goodbye to tour manager Jack Carson and thanked him for allowing me to hang, before goodbyes to Patrick, Todd and Chris. I walked off up the street as their vehicles rolled out.

I rang Stevie D to see where he was and he was also heading back to the car park. After bumping into an old friend Nick Hatton for a quick chat, I piled into the only remaining seat in Stevie D's packed car as we headed towards the city. Everyone was buzzing from the concert; most saying they'd go so far as to say it was the best they'd ever seen.

After stopping for some food, we went to Wazza's house. I phoned Corey to see if he was going to kick on but he wasn't, so we arranged to meet at the airport the next morning at 11am for a drink before I headed home. I caught up on some missed calls as the others sat around the hazy lounge room with a bong. I was not keen on sitting around the bachelors' pad all night, instead keen to head into the city to see some of Tommy Lee's DJ event.

Steve and I soon left them to it and ventured to Capitol nightclub. I gave him a VIP pass and after some confusion at the door, we were finally allowed free entry. As another DJ played, we walked around the up-market venue to see if we knew anyone else.

I was soon approached by a young guy who was apologising to me. With the loud doof-doof consuming my head, I was at first confused by what he was saying and wondering what he had done to me. Turns out he was one of the fans that were at Fremantle Cemetery yesterday.

I asked him if he tailed us from the airport. He said he did go to the airport hoping to see the band but then they headed back towards their home down Fremantle way when the band left from the tarmac. Driving along Leach Highway half an hour later, he said he noticed the black Statesman we were in and recognised it from the airport. Just then we turned off the highway into Carrington Street and he said he figured we were going to Bon's grave, so they just waited near our car for us to come back.

Steve and I had a couple of drinks, noticing that there were a lot of lovely looking ladies in the place. Former football player and B-grade celebrity Warrick Capper walked through the crowd with a blonde, as each group of people they passed then whispered to each other and laughed behind their backs.

Pedro soon arrived and we chatted for a bit, as Kimo came up from behind and bear hugged me before wandering upstairs. Tommy Lee then came through the crowd to the DJ booth, with his security guy Earl Gabbidon, assistant Tony Sullivan, and Mighty Mike in his super hero costume, as the message came over the PA that no photographs were to be taken.

When I last saw Tommy DJ it was at the end of his set in Melbourne, so it was good to see the beginning of his set this time around. As he worked the crowd with dance beats pumping, we sat and watched, taking it all in for half-an-hour or an hour. Mighty Mike had a separate stage that he shared with a couple of dancers from the club. He entertained the crowd with his dancing, interspersed with various break-dancing moves, acrobatic moves and bodybuilding poses.

Steve had well and truly had enough of the music and was ready to go home, so I said that I just wanted to say goodbye to some people first. I couldn't see Kimo or Pedro so we headed over towards the DJ booth. As Earl was focused on crowd control, I gave Tommy a wave and salute goodbye. Mighty Mike stopped his dancing when I waved goodbye, coming to the edge of the stage to give me a sweaty hug and tell me that it had been great fun hanging out. I told him to take care and that we'd keep in touch.

As we left the club and headed back to Stevie D's, he was telling me how the bass frequencies were hurting his ears when we were on the dance floor to say farewells. It was probably 2am when we got back to his home and I was beat. As I talked with Steve and Mel about the festival and club experiences of the day, I laid down and crashed.

Paul says, 'On with the Show'

Motley Crue's biggest fan gets to live his rock 'n' roll dream

Andrew McManus & 96fm present
ROCK & ROLL SHOW
BLACKJACK
Claremont Showgrounds
Saturday Dec 10 2005
5.00pm - 10.00pm
Claremont Showgrounds Main Arena
18+ ID REQUIRED FOR ENTRY
NO BYO - NO PASS OUTS
See rear of this ticket for conditions of entry.
COMP794
www.ampresents.com
COMP794
FULL SHOW DETAILS:
www.heatseeker.com.au

CARNIVAL OF SINS
MÖTLEY CRÜE
VIP
FINAL 1 X

ROCK'N'ROLL SHOW
BLACKJACK
Starring
MÖTLEY CRÜE
The LIVING END
MOTORHEAD
FIREBALLS
The CASANOVAS
DAY OF THE DEAD
SATURDAY
DECEMBER
10
CLAREMONT SHOWGROUNDS MAIN ARENA
TICKETS ON SALE TOMORROW!!

FUCK
FUCK

nikki
sixx
InTuneGP
FICK
DICK
nikki
sixx
InTuneGP
FUCK
OFF

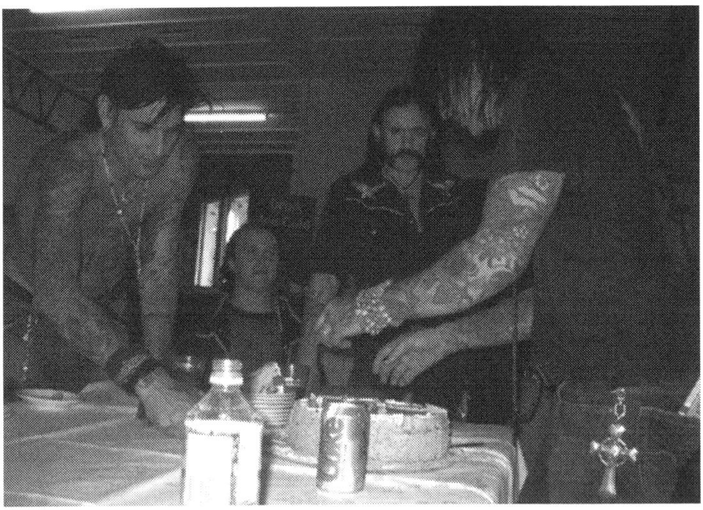

MAYHEM

Sunday, December 11, 2005 - Perth to Melbourne

My alarm soon went off, as it was time to rise and get ready to head back home to Melbourne. Steve and Mel dropped me at the domestic Perth Airport and we said our goodbyes. As it was just after 11am, I phoned Corey to see where he was. I woke him up but he said he would get ready and still meet me for that drink before my flight scheduled for 12:25pm.

I checked-in and headed for the bar, opting for a coffee instead of something alcoholic. As I drank my latte, Patrick from Andrew McManus Presents walked by so we had a brief chat about the tour. I soon headed to the boarding gate and saw that my flight was delayed by half-an-hour. I thought I'd be able to kill some of that time catching up with Corey some more, but he never arrived and I've still not heard from him; maybe he went back to sleep.

When my 2,703km return flight finally got off the ground, I sat in my seat, closed my eyes and reflected on all the events of the past week. Before the tour, I prepared a heap of questions that I wanted to ask the guys, but when I was on tour I didn't want to be considered a pesky reporter hassling them all the time. It was most important to me that I just hung out and had some fun with them as much as I could.

After being a fan for fifteen years and knowing the amount of daily effort over the last decade I had put into my works on the band; just to finally see them play a live concert in front of me was a dream come true. My Australian tour had taken me to see all six concerts in eight days – awesome! But it turned out to be so much more than that.

I'm not sure how my week could have been any better really. It certainly exceeded all my expectations. The band had complimented me during their press conference, I had a song dedicated to me in front of 9,000 people in the band's first show on Australian shores in fifteen years, I was given a smashed bass – now signed, I was given personal clothing from the band, I was front row – side of stage – backstage, I was fed – I was drunk – I was covered in blood, I traveled with the band from concerts to hotels to airports, I made lots of friends for life, and I have lots of photos (and a scar on my hand) to help savour the fond memories. Wow! It started sinking in. So much happened this week that I could write a book on it.

I thought about my Mötley journey over the years; from my wife first introducing me to their Too Fast For Love album, to then starting my website that gave me a reason to communicate with the band members and their management, to consistently growing my profile and credibility over the years with quality works both on and for the band, to how that massive amount of hard work then allowed me to venture inside the band's inner sanctum and experience things that a typical fan never could… priceless experiences that money can't buy, nor can be bid for on eBay. I felt proud of what I had achieved; I felt satisfied.

I opened my eyes. Was it all a dream? Perhaps. I looked out of the aeroplane's window at the clouds. I was on cloud nine.

It was after 7pm when the plane touched down and I was keen to get home. The guys from The Casanovas were on the same flight back to Melbourne, so I said goodbye to them at the carousels as they waited for their luggage, before heading outside for my bus into the city.

My wife Sara met me at the station and we drove home, where I shared the latest stories of my adventure with my family. I was asked what it was like hanging out with Nikki, the cool rock star celebrity. I thought for a second and tried to convey, "Yes, he is that, but to me, it feels like he is one of the most caring and thoughtful friends I have in this world."

Time for sleep, I knew it would be back to the realities of my bill-paying nine-to-five job tomorrow morning.

As the circus curtains were finally drawn to end my tour, Nikki soon posted a picture of us together on his www.nikkisixx.net website with the caption:

"ME AND PAUL MILES IN BRISBANE. HE TRAVELED AROUND AUSTRALIA WITH US AND WE REALLY GOT TO KNOW EACH OTHER WELL, HE AND HIS WIFE ARE FANTASTIC PEOPLE. HE HAS DONE AN AMAZING JOB WITH THE CHRONOLOGICAL CRUE WEBSITE, BUT MORE IMPORTANTLY, HES JUST GREAT PEOPLE."

It was a lovely way to cap off the tour.

Thank you Nikki. Thank you Mötley Crüe. Thank you to the Crüe's crew. Thank you to the guys in Motörhead and all the other support bands. Thank you to the Crüeheads down under. See you all again next tour across Australia!

Long live rock 'n' roll. Long live Mötley fucking Crüe!

FRIENDS
PHOTOS BY
N. SIXX

Photo Guide & Credits

P19: Paul Miles and Tommy Lee on the 'black carpet' at The 2005 Jack Awards. Photo by Paul Miles

P20, top: Jack Awards invitation, displaying the front on the left and the reverse side on the right.

P20, bottom: Petrina Convey of Universal Music Australia with Paul Miles at The 2005 Jack Awards. Photo by Paul Miles.

P21: Tommy Lee being interviewed on the 'black carpet' on arrival at The 2005 Jack Awards by Yumi Stynes and Danny Clayton of Channel V.

P22, top: Paul Miles holding Grinspoon's heavy Jack Award at the after-show cocktail party. Photo by Rosemary Milsom.

P22, bottom: Chris Cheney from The Living End and Paul Miles at The 2005 Jack Awards after-show cocktail party. Photo by Paul Miles.

P23, top: Drummers Kram from Spiderbait and Ben Gillies from Silverchair singing Kickstart My Heart to Paul Miles at The 2005 Jack Awards after-show cocktail party. Photo by Paul Miles.

P23, bottom: Sarah McLeod from The Superjesus and Paul Miles in the wee small hours after The 2005 Jack Awards. Photo by Paul Miles.

P24, top: Tour artwork proof for DL promotional card, displaying the front on the left and the reverse side on the right with "Nikki Six".

P24, bottom: Street poster promoting the first Melbourne concert on December 6.

P25: Tommy Love from The Casanovas holding Paul Miles. Photo by Dean Boswell.

P39: Invitation to Mötley Crüe's press conference at Sydney's InterContinental hotel.

P40: During and conclusion of Mötley Crüe's press conference at Sydney's InterContinental hotel on Friday,

December 2, 2005. Photos by Craig Redfearn of Universal Music Australia.

P52: Scan of ticket issued to Paul Miles for Sydney concert.

P53, top: Mötley Crüe All Access laminate tour pass issued to Paul Miles, displaying the front on the left and the reverse side on the right.

P53, bottom: Nikki Sixx and Paul Miles hanging out backstage in Nikki's Sydney dressing room, following Paul's first-ever Mötley Crüe concert. Photo by Shinbone Starr.

P65: Paul Miles with Nikki Sixx backstage in Brisbane, minutes before the Crüe hit the stage. Photo by Paul Miles.

P66, top: Scan of ticket issued to Paul Miles for Brisbane concert.

P66, bottom: Scan of bright orange VIP pass issued to Paul Miles for Brisbane concert

P67: Scan of production run-sheet, souvenired from backstage wall after the Brisbane concert.

P78: Shinbone Starr, Mighty Mike, and Paul Miles in foyer of Crown Promenade hotel in Melbourne. Photo by Sara Miles.

P86: Support band laminate tour pass issued to Sara Miles, displaying the front side.

P87, top: Scan of ticket issued to Paul Miles for first Melbourne concert, as well as another ticket below that was passed out by door staff after the show.

P87, bottom: Sara Miles, Nikki Sixx, and Paul Miles backstage in Nikki's Melbourne dressing room, before Sara's first-ever Mötley Crüe concert. Photo by Shinbone Starr.

P88: Sara Miles and Paul Miles backstage at Melbourne's Vodafone Arena. Photos and PhotoShop manipulation by Nikki Sixx.

P89: Nikki Sixx's smashed bass from Melbourne concert, given to Paul Miles during show. Strap signed later on the tour in Perth. Photo by Paul Miles.

P90: Rick Davies with Nikki Sixx backstage in Nikki's dressing room after the Melbourne concert. Photo by Paul Miles.

P96: Marquee of Melbourne's Palais Theatre before the show. Photo by Paul Miles.

P97, top: Scan of house ticket purchased by Paul Miles for second Melbourne concert.

P97, bottom: Scan of bright orange VIP pass issued to Paul Miles for second Melbourne concert.

P98, top: Pre-show entertainment as Mighty Mike rides his unicycle up the side-street next to Melbourne's Palais Theatre, with Airbourne members behind him. Photo by Jason Mayne.

P98, bottom: Scan of my Vince Neil guitar plectrum obtained during the Melbourne Palais concert, displaying his signature on one side and the Red, White & Crüe girl on the other.

P99: Scan of production run-sheet, souvenired from backstage wall after the Melbourne Palais concert. Note the silver hearts, drawn as paint marker pens were tested by production staff prior to the band signing various items.

P100: Scan of production band identification sheet, souvenired from backstage wall after the Melbourne Palais concert.

P101, top: Jozie Di Maria, Sara Miles, and Paul Miles in the back of a taxi in Melbourne city. Photo by Paul Miles.

P101, bottom: Paul Miles and Jozie Di Maria on the dance floor at Melbourne's Cherry bar. Photos by Jason Mayne.

P102: Paul Miles and Jozie Di Maria under the AC/DC Lane street sign in Melbourne city. Photo by Sara Miles.

P103: Tommy Lee DJing at The Loft in Melbourne. Photo by Paul Miles.

P104: Tommy Lee DJing at The Loft in Melbourne. Photo by Paul Miles.

P105, top: Tommy Lee swigging from a Jagermeister bottle as he DJs at The Loft in Melbourne. Photo by Paul Miles.

P105, bottom: Alecia and Paul Miles in the DJ booth at The Loft in Melbourne. Photo by Paul Miles.

P106, top: DJ Aero and Tommy Lee perform at The Loft in Melbourne. Photo by Paul Miles.

P106, bottom: Mighty Mike working the crowd in his superhero costume as Tommy Lee DJs at The Loft in Melbourne. Photo by Paul Miles.

P107: The sweaty, hard-working Mighty Mike in the DJ booth at The Loft in Melbourne. Photo by Paul Miles.

P108: Mighty Mike wants you! The Loft in Melbourne. Photo by Paul Miles.

P116: Scan of bright pink VIP pass issued to Paul Miles for Adelaide concert.

P117, top: Scan of ticket issued to Paul Miles for Adelaide concert.

P117, bottom: Scan of the Qantas boarding pass for the flight of Mr. Nikki Sixx from Melbourne to Adelaide, and given to Paul Miles backstage after Adelaide concert by Nikki.

P118, top: Mikkey Dee from Motörhead, Nikki's security guard Kimo, Lemmy Kilmister from Motörhead, and Tommy Lee's security guard Earl Gabbidon, backstage in Adelaide before Motörhead's set. Photo by Paul Miles.

P118, bottom: A Motörhead road-case backstage in Adelaide. Photo by Paul Miles.

P119, top: Motörhead set-list from Adelaide concert. The X's denote the songs played that night.

P119, bottom: Mötley Crüe dancer Jozie Di Maria filming Motörhead's set in Adelaide from the side of stage, wearing her pink slippers. Photo by Paul Miles.

P120: It's slippers off and boots on as Jozie Di Maria finishes getting into her stage costume in her dressing room backstage in Adelaide. Photo by Paul Miles.

P121: Jozie Di Maria captures more backstage action on her video camera in Adelaide. Photo by Paul Miles.

P122, top: Nikki Sixx's bass tech Darron Meeks and Paul Miles. Photo by Paul Miles.

P122, bottom: Darron Meeks in his base at the side of stage, prior to the Crüe's show in Adelaide. Note Nikki Sixx's bottle of fake blood on top of the case. Photo by Paul Miles.

P123: Darron Meeks in his overalls and tuning Nikki Sixx's bass guitars before the Adelaide concert. Photo by Paul Miles.

P124, top: The rack of Nikki Sixx bass guitars, pres-show in Adelaide. Photo by Paul Miles.

P124, bottom: Pedro Pineda and Paul Miles in Adelaide. Photo by Paul Miles.

P125, top: Mighty Mike in his Adelaide dressing room pre-show. Photo by Paul Miles.

P125, bottom: Kimo and Nikki Sixx outside Nikki's dressing room as show time draws near in Adelaide. Photo by Paul Miles.

P126, top: Nikki Sixx and Paul Miles backstage before the Crüe hits the stage in Adelaide, taken on one of Nikki's toy cameras. Photo by Kimo.

P126, bottom: Lemmy Kilmister and a towelled-up Mikkey Dee from Motörhead with Nikki Sixx, backstage corridor in between sets in Adelaide. Photo by Paul Miles.

P127, top: Lemmy Kilmister and Nikki Sixx - dubbed the 'Killed By Breath' shot. Photo by Paul Miles.

P127, bottom: Mick Mars being led up the narrow rear stage ramp by his security guard Rhyno as Mötley Crüe was about to hit the stage in Adelaide. Photo by Paul Miles.

P128: Mighty Mike walks the backstage corridors towards the stage to commence the Mötley Crüe show in Adelaide. Photo by Paul Miles.

P129: Mötley Crüe set-list stuck to stage railing in Adelaide. Photo by Paul Miles.

P130: Nikki Sixx and Paul Miles backstage in Nikki's Adelaide dressing room after the Crüe's concert. Photo by Kimo.

P131: Paul Miles with Nikki's stage hat and leather jacket on in Nikki's Adelaide dressing room. Photo by Nikki Sixx.

P132: Four exposure toy camera snap of Paul Miles in Nikki Sixx's Adelaide dressing room. Photo by Nikki Sixx.

P133: Kimo about to eat a peanut butter and jelly sandwich in Nikki Sixx's Adelaide dressing room. Photo by Paul Miles.

P134: Elbow seam of Nikki Sixx's leather jacket that was given to Paul Miles backstage after the Adelaide concert. Photo by Paul Miles.

P146: Nikki Sixx and Paul Miles in the back of a chauffeur-driven vehicle heading from Hyatt hotel to Adelaide airport. Nikki's four-exposure toy camera sits on his lap. Photo by Paul Miles.

P147, top: Nikki Sixx photographing the plaque on Bon Scott's memorial seat at Fremantle Cemetery. Photo by Paul Miles.

P147, bottom: Nikki Sixx sits on Bon Scott's memorial seat at Fremantle Cemetery. Bon's resting plaque can be seen on the ground behind, decorated with an Australian flag and beer can. Photo by Paul Miles.

P148, top: Nikki Sixx photographing Jozie Di Maria against Bon Scott's memorial seat at Fremantle Cemetery. Photo by Paul Miles.

P148, bottom: Kimo photographing the plaque on Bon Scott's memorial seat at Fremantle Cemetery. Photo by Paul Miles.

P149: Scan of the cover of rough draft copy of the manuscript to *The Dirt*, signed to Paul Miles by Nikki Sixx in Perth hotel room.

P150: Scan of an email message sent by Nikki Sixx to Paul Miles in December 1995, signed to Paul Miles by Nikki Sixx in Perth hotel room a decade later.

P151: Three images showing the guitar strap signed to Paul Miles in Nikki's room at Perth's Hyatt hotel.

P164, top: Stevie D and Paul Miles on scooters in Perth. Photo by Mel Dick.

P164, bottom: Scan of an article from one of Perth's newspapers. (You can read the text on p153)

P165, top: Scan of ticket issued to Paul Miles for Perth's Blackjack festival.

P165, bottom: Scan of light orange VIP pass issued to Paul Miles for Perth's Blackjack festival.

P166: Scan of street-press poster advertising Perth's Blackjack festival.

P167, top: Some of Nikki Sixx's stage clothes laid out on a chair in his Perth dressing room. Photo by Paul Miles.

P167, bottom: Nikki Sixx preparing the 'Killed By Breath' photo for upload to his website, in his dressing room pre-show in Perth. Photo by Paul Miles.

P168: Mikkey Dee from Motörhead on stage in Perth. Shot with no zoom. Photo by Paul Miles.

P169: Lemmy Kilmister from Motörhead on stage in Perth. Again, shot with no zoom. Perhaps the booming sound caused the camera to vibrate. Photo by Paul Miles.

P170, top: Mikkey Dee from Motörhead and Paul, side of Mötley's stage in Perth before encore. Photo by Paul Miles.

P170, bottom: Lemmy and Vince Neil, side of Mötley's stage in Perth before encore with both bands. Vince is running through the lyrics to Anarchy in the U.K. hoping Lemmy will recall them. Photo by Paul Miles.

P171, top: Lemmy being led off stage in Perth by security guard Earl Gabbidon with Jozie Di Maria in the background. Photo by Paul Miles.

P171, bottom: Two Nikki Sixx plectrums, displaying one side on left and the reverse side on the right.

P172, top: Nikki Sixx blowing out his candles on a cake held by Basia, with Tommy Lee whistling in the background. Photo by Paul Miles.

P172, bottom: Nikki Sixx serving up his birthday cake to Tommy Lee with Mighty Mike and Lemmy Kilmister waiting for their pieces. Photo by Paul Miles.

P173: Paul Miles and Mick Mars backstage in Perth after the concert. Photo by Rhyno.

P174: Paul Miles and Lemmy Kilmister backstage in Perth after the concert. Photo by Jozie Di Maria.

P175: Paul Miles and Tommy Lee backstage in Perth after the concert. Photo by Jozie Di Maria.

P180: CD of photos given to Paul Miles by Nikki Sixx.

P190: Paul Miles at Melbourne's Crown Promenade hotel during the tour, celebrating a huge 2005! Photo by Sara Miles.

Paul
thank you
for everything
Nikki Sixx

About the Author

Paul Miles is the world's #1 Mötley Crüe historian, documenting the facts behind the band's "sex, drugs & rock'n'roll" lifestyle since 1995.

The pages of his acclaimed Chronological Crue website have been read well-over four million times, following its launch on January 27, 1997 – the day vocalist Vince Neil re-united with the Crüe on stage at the American Music Awards.

Chronological Crue has been featured in many newspapers and publications around the world, including Japan's *Bass Magazine*, *Penthouse* magazine, hard rockers' favourite *Metal Edge*, and even the band's own Electronic Press Kit.

MTV & VH1 have both drawn upon and credited the site for their production of TV programs on Mötley Crüe, while music industry journalists and critics continue to use his works as an invaluable reference on the band.

Paul Miles was Executive Producer of the award-winning, worlds-first Mötley Crüe tribute CD, released with a Global Broadcast Premiere on the world's largest online radio station. Later in 1999, Miles was honoured to write the liner notes inside Mötley Crüe's first-ever live album - *Live: Entertainment or Death.*

After unsuccessfully pitching to band management the idea of turning his history content into a book a few years earlier, Paul Miles was engaged in 2001 to analytically assess the manuscript of the band's autobiography as it was in production.

The Dirt then spent a record amount of time on the New York Times Bestseller List, and the infamous story is being turned into a big-screen Hollywood movie by Paramount Pictures and MTV Films. Miles has since given assistance to the movie's screenwriter in verifying the accuracy of the script.

Paul Miles lives in Melbourne, Australia with his wife and children, and when he's not in front of his computer updating fans with all the latest Mötley happenings, he can be found in the city's many bars and clubs as an entertaining rock DJ.

2005

"As the minutes fade away, I can't remember, have I said all I can say?
You're my everything; you make me feel so alive."

If I Die Tomorrow, Mötley Crüe, 2005.

Have you got these other rock'n'roll books by Paul Miles?

Sex Tips From Rock Stars
In Their Own Words
www.SexTipsFromRockStars.com

Before I Hit The Stage
Rock'n'Roll Moments in New York City
www.BeforeIHitTheStage.com

Printed in Great Britain
by Amazon

72291265R00121